Praise for *Developing Women Leaders*

"In any organization today, women leaders will help drive business growth and improved performance. Anna Marie Valerio's *Developing Women Leaders* is a practical guide that helps organizations not only to achieve this growth objective, but also to create the right opportunities for talented women to develop their careers and to advance within that company."

Nancy McKinstry, Chief Executive Officer and
Chairman of the Executive Board, Wolters Kluwer

"Dr. Valerio's thoughtful and thought-provoking book is essential reading for anyone who cares about the development of the next generation of leaders, regardless of gender. As a female president and CEO in a historically male-dominated industry, I recognize the value and insights offered in the book, and applaud the proactive approaches to gender issues in the workplace."

Nancy Hill, President-CEO,
American Association of Advertising Agencies

"*Developing Women Leaders* is a trove of useful advice for the advancement of women. Many talented women whose careers have stalled at mid-management can apply the book's strategies to move into top-level careers. Women and men benefit when we have the most talented people leading organizations. Valerio offers something for everyone. There are great 'tips' for women who want to advance their careers, administrators who control access to the top, and for human resource departments that can help to increase the number of women in leadership positions."

Diane F. Halpern, Claremont McKenna College

D1319542

Talent Management Essentials

Series Editor: Steven G. Rogelberg, Ph.D.
Professor and Director Organizational Science, University of North Carolina – Charlotte

Senior Advisory Board:
Eric Elder, Ph.D., Director, Talent Management, Corning Incorporated
William H. Macey, Ph.D., Chief Executive Officer, Valtera Corporation
Cindy McCauley, Ph.D., Senior Fellow, Center for Creative Leadership
Elaine D. Pulakos, Ph.D., Chief Operating Officer, PDRI, A PreVisor Company
Douglas H. Reynolds, Ph.D., Vice President, Assessment Technology, Development
Dimensions International
Ann Marie Ryan, Ph.D., Professor, Michigan State University
Lise Saari, Ph.D., Director, Global Workforce Research, IBM
John Scott, Ph.D., Vice President, Applied Psychological Techniques, Inc.
Dean Stamoulis, Ph.D., Managing Director, Global Executive Assessment Practice,
Russell Reynolds Associates

Special Features

Each volume contains a host of actual case studies, sample materials, tips, and
cautionary notes. Issues pertaining to globalization, technology, and key executive points
are highlighted throughout.

Titles in the Talent Management Essentials series:

Performance Management: A New Approach for Driving Business Results
Elaine D. Pulakos

Designing and Implementing Global Selection Systems
Ann Marie Ryan and Nancy T. Tippins

Designing Workplace Mentoring Programs: An Evidence-Based Approach
Tammy D. Allen, Lisa M. Finkelstein, and Mark L. Poteet

Career Paths: Charting Courses to Success for Organizations and Their Employees
Gary W. Carter, Kevin W. Cook, and David W. Dorsey

Mistreatment in the Workplace: Prevention and Resolution for Managers and Organizations
Julie B. Olson-Buchanan and Wendy R. Boswell

Developing Women Leaders: A Guide for Men and Women in Organizations
Anna Marie Valerio

Employee Engagement: Tools for Analysis, Practice, and Competitive Advantage
William H. Macey, Benjamin Schneider, Karen M. Barbera, and Scott A. Young

Online Recruiting and Selection: Innovations in Talent Acquisition
Douglas H. Reynolds and John A. Weiner

Senior Executive Assessment: A Key to Responsible Corporate Governance
Dean Stamoulis

Real Time Leadership Development
Paul R. Yost and Mary Mannion Plunkett

Developing Women Leaders

A Guide for Men and Women in Organizations

Anna Marie Valerio

 **WILEY-BLACKWELL**

A John Wiley & Sons, Ltd., Publication

This edition first published 2009
© 2009 Anna Marie Valerio

Blackwell Publishing was acquired by John Wiley & Sons in February 2007. Blackwell's publishing program has been merged with Wiley's global Scientific, Technical, and Medical business to form Wiley-Blackwell.

Registered Office
John Wiley & Sons Ltd, The Atrium, Southern Gate, Chichester, West Sussex, PO19 8SQ, United Kingdom

Editorial Offices
350 Main Street, Malden, MA 02148-5020, USA
9600 Garsington Road, Oxford, OX4 2DQ, UK
The Atrium, Southern Gate, Chichester, West Sussex, PO19 8SQ, UK

For details of our global editorial offices, for customer services, and for information about how to apply for permission to reuse the copyright material in this book please see our website at www.wiley.com/wiley-blackwell.

The right of Anna Marie Valerio to be identified as the author of this work has been asserted in accordance with the Copyright, Designs and Patents Act 1988.

Library of Congress Cataloging-in-Publication Data

Valerio, Anna Marie
  Developing women leaders : a guide for men and women in organizations / Anna Marie Valerio.
      p. cm. – (Talent management essentials)
  Includes bibliographical references and index.
  ISBN 978-1-4051-8371-0 (hardcover : alk. paper) – ISBN 978-1-4051-8370-3 (pbk. : alk. paper)
1. Women executives. 2. Leadership. I. Title. II. Series.
  HD6054.3.V34 2009
  658.4′092082–dc22

                                                                              2008051196

A catalogue record for this book is available from the British Library.

Icon in Case Scenario boxes © Kathy Konkle/istockphoto.com

Set in 10.5 on 12.5 pt Minion by SNP Best-set Typesetter Ltd., Hong Kong
Printed in Singapore by Ho Printing Singapore Pte Ltd

1 2009

Dedication

With love and gratitude to my mother, Fernanda, and to the memory of my father, Nicholas, both of whom imbued in me a love of learning and fostered my educational achievement.

To my cousin, Angela, and to the memory of my aunts, Mary, Anna, Margaret, and my cousin Anna, whose pride in my accomplishments I will always cherish.

Contents

Series Editor's Preface

The *Talent Management Essentials* series presents state-of-the-art thinking on critical talent management topics ranging from global staffing, to career pathing, to engagement, to executive staffing, to performance management, to mentoring, to real-time leadership development. Authored by leading authorities and scholars on their respective topics, each volume offers state-of-the-art thinking and the epitome of evidence-based practice. These authors bring to their books an incredible wealth of experience working with small, large, public, and private organizations, as well as keen insights into the science and best practices associated with talent management.

Written succinctly and without superfluous "fluff," this series provides powerful and practical treatments of essential talent topics critical to maximizing individual and organizational health, well-being, and effectiveness. The books, taken together, provide a comprehensive and contemporary treatment of approaches, tools, and techniques associated with Talent Management. The goal of the series is to produce focused, prescriptive volumes that translate the data- and practice-based knowledge of organizational psychology, human resources management, and organizational behavior into practical, "how to" advice for dealing with cutting-edge organizational issues and problems.

Talent Management Essentials is a comprehensive, practitioner-oriented series of "best practices" for the busy solution-oriented manager, executive, HR leader, and consultant. And, in its application of evidence-based practice, this series will also appeal to professors, executive MBA students, and graduate students in Organizational Behavior, Human Resources Management, and I/O Psychology.

Steven Rogelberg

Preface

This book grew from initial conversations several years ago with a colleague who pointed out to me that my background provided me with a unique vantage point from which to explore the topic of women's leadership. My background as a psychologist, my prior leadership roles in Fortune 500 companies, and my current work as an executive coach in independent practice all provided me with advantages for examining and writing about these issues. The collection of my professional experiences has contributed to my knowledge base, shaped my approach to the topic of women's leadership, and positioned me well for this effort.

I started doing interviews with people in Fortune 500 companies and universities to hear what was in their minds and hearts. At the first interviews I was surprised by the degree of excitement expressed by the interviewees. "Keep going with this – we all need to learn more!" was the unanimous response. When my clients and their bosses learned about this endeavor, they expressed the same sentiments. At professional meetings I began presenting programs, creating panel discussions involving colleagues, and wrote articles on the subject of developing women leaders. The outpouring of enthusiastic responses I received for this work from executives, colleagues, graduate students, and others further spurred me onward. My efforts culminate in this book.

During the past thirty to forty years we Americans have witnessed a seismic shift in our views of women as adults and as leaders. Back then "the girls" were channeled into the study of school teaching, nursing, and social work. Airline stewardesses were dismissed when they got married. Although women's career advancement has evolved slowly, we now have women as senators, governors, and corporate CEOs. Women fight in wars and fly into space. These are no longer "remarkable" events. The tide hasn't fully turned, but the trends are clear. The day will come when we won't have to discuss "gender roles" when we talk about women as leaders. Right now, however, we do.

Behavioral scientists have been tracking this shift, chasing away myths and folklore with solid research information. Much of that information has been in scientific journals and books, is hard to read, and even harder to apply. This book tries to bring the best information to light, and do so in a readable, organized way.

In my work as an executive coach I am privileged to have the trust of talented women and men who share their feelings about being "high achievers" in their worlds of work and personal life. Theirs is not an easy journey. It seems to me that both men and women can benefit from open discussion and dialogue about the influence of gender and gender roles on leadership. Fortunately, social science research provides us with some answers on both gender similarities and differences in leadership and the influence of gender roles. It is time for managers and others in organizations – men and women together – to discuss gender issues and to arrive at better solutions for all. It is a topic that touches men and women alike, as many of us have been influenced by the experiences of our mothers, aunts, and sisters and have heard the stories of our grandmothers and great-grandmothers. For the most part, the stories describe their hard work in order to make things better for the next generation.

As a woman and as a professional, it has been an especially personal task to write this book. I hope that it will not be read with a sense of detachment, but rather with a feeling of wonder at how we as a society have struggled upward over these years. These feelings should motivate you to create change in your own life, in your organizations, and in your communities. This is not a novel, yet it is a story of our lives, our relatives' and neighbors' lives – based on good science applied to real people in real organizations. It is a status report of the dialogue about women and leadership. Such a conversation reflects every aspect of our society – business, government, families, careers, health, law – and our collective view of merit, fairness, and social parity.

My hope is that by facing these issues together, women and men will arrive at solutions that will create organizations and societies that serve us better, whatever our role or gender. And, yes, that *our* hard work will make it easier for the next generation of women to pursue leadership.

Book Overview

The topic of Developing Women Leaders has many stakeholders and many audiences who need to know about it. The book is meant to be a practical, user-friendly guide for women and men in organizations. It is designed to appeal to a very broad audience of people in organizations interested in developing the leadership capacities of women. This audience may include women, men, their bosses, Human Resource (HR) executives and professionals, CEOs, their top leadership teams, and others seeking to make informed decisions for themselves and their organizations regarding leadership development for women.

What You Will Learn

There is something in this book for everyone interested in the topic of leadership. Some chapters are written for the entire audience. Three chapters are addressed to CEOs and HR executives, managers, and women, respectively. CEOs and HR executives may discover new solutions implemented by some best-practice organizations on the forefront of leadership development. Male and female bosses will acquire practical tips and suggestions to help them improve their own leadership and manage talent in their groups. Women will learn what actions they can take to be proactive in their own development. All stakeholders will gain insights from the chapter containing five first-hand accounts written by successful women about their leadership experiences: defining moments, obstacles overcome, lessons learned.

The conclusions and recommended actions offered in the book rest upon the strongest social science research findings on the behaviors that contribute to effective leadership. The book emphasizes what men and women need to know about leadership research and development in the areas of leadership competencies, personality, leadership styles, and stereotypical perceptions of gender. It explains development options such as job assignments, coaching, mentoring, and formal development programs and the pertinent research results associated with each. Throughout the book the comments from high-achieving men and women interviewed by the author provide thoughtful, real-world commentary.

Audience

This book is intended for men and women in multiple audiences: those in management in both for-profit and non-profit organizations who are interested in developing talented women; those male and female executives and managers interested in advancing their female direct reports; and those who wish to learn to work better with their female bosses, women executives, and managers who would like to enhance their own job performance. Both HR and line professionals charged with the direct responsibility of managing corporate talent may find it helpful. Indeed, some parts of this book may be of interest to those in other organizational roles, such as the direct reports and peers of talented women. This book will also appeal to the young women and men who are just starting their careers with the hope and expectation of learning from each other and meeting the daunting challenges that they face in today's organizations. When finished with the book, readers should be able to use the information to better carry out their work objectives in their jobs. Ultimately, the development of women leaders will improve organizational capability and financial performance, and lead to greater teamwork and job satisfaction for both the men and women in today's organizations. The book focuses primarily on people in U.S. organizations, where much of the underlying research has taken place. However, some of the thoughts and suggestions in this book may apply beyond the American culture to spark some creative ideas in organizations that originate in other cultural contexts.

The topic of developing women leaders has relevance across the range of all organizations, including Fortune 500 companies, government, academic institutions, non-profit organizations, and small businesses. Hence, the book targets a very large audience and hopes to bridge the gap between the valuable findings from scholarly research and the people who stand to benefit from it the most. As you turn the pages of this book, here are some things to look for:

- *For women*: This book will provide you with insights on how to take responsibility for your own development, advance your own career and that of other talented women. You will find ideas and suggestions for actions you can take to give yourself the experiences that will enhance your growth as a leader.
- *For men*: If you are curious about how to develop women as leaders, this book will have tips for you. Many men confront these challenges, and this book will help you think it through. Because a large percentage of what we know about leadership development is the same for men as for women, as you think about what you need to develop talented women you will also be helping talented men as well. Armed with the knowledge in this book, you will have greater insights into your own behavior and how to grow as a leader.
- *For CEOs and HR executives*: As chief stewards of the organization's mission and strategy, you occupy a unique role in building your organization's capability. The power and influence of your business decisions can have ramifications for years to come and the human resource policies and practices implemented under your watch can affect all stakeholders. In recent years your number one issue has been talent management and you recognize that talented people are your most valuable asset. This book will help you meet the overall needs of your organization as you encourage *all* of your employees to flourish by using their talents and skills for the sake of the enterprise and for that of themselves and their families.
- *For the bosses of women*: You play a pivotal role in developing the talent in your organization. As you know, helping your staff solve performance problems and develop their individual potential is a central aspect of your responsibilities to them and to your employer. This book will help you with those tasks by enabling you identify the things that only you can do to contribute to the successful performance of the women who report to you. At the same time, of course, you build the capability of your organization.
- *For HR professionals*: You will find ideas for creating or enhancing Human Resource programs, policies, and practices to attract, retain, and develop talented women in your organization. This book will also help you influence key decision-makers and communicate to others how developing women leaders can add momentum to the overall diversity initiatives in your organization. The book will also

assist you in your important role as an HR professional in helping the managers in your organization.

- *For coaches and their clients*: You coach people about work behaviors that will increase their success on the job. The knowledge in this book will allow you to better manage the coaching engagement and to help your clients manage the requirements of their jobs in a proactive, productive way. In addition, this book could be used as a recommended read for your clients and their managers when you perceive the need for greater understanding of women managers and their developmental needs.
- *For researchers*: Because this book is written for an audience whose knowledge of the social science literature ranges from little or none to expert or Ph.D. level and beyond, it is written in more of a "friendly," vernacular voice, rather than a scholarly, scientific one. The research studies published on the topics that pertain to women's leadership number in the thousands and it would be impossible to include all of them in this volume. Rather, this book takes the strongest research findings from a number of different disciplines and topic areas and incorporates it into a foundation for the ideas and suggestions offered here. The Notes section at the end of the book will provide you with the references for further reading.

Author's Interviews

This book attempts to offer practical solutions that rest on a solid research foundation. Blended into this mix are the views of women and men in today's organizations taken from forty interviews conducted from 2006 to 2008 by the author with high achievers in major U.S. companies and universities. In the text they are identified as "interviewee" or with a position title such as "vice president." They were interviewed with the understanding that 1) the book was aimed at helping managers and organizations develop women leaders, and 2) their remarks would not be attributed to them. These conditions allowed them to speak truthfully about their personal experiences and their views on the potentially controversial topic of the influence of gender on women's leadership development. Some of the results from the initial interviews were summarized and published by the author in a brief article.[1] As explained below, in Parts II and III the interviewees' ideas about what they believe can be done to develop and advance talented women lend a supportive voice and vitality to the research findings and recommendations.

How Is This Book Different?

In comparison to other books on the market, this book presents research-based, practical solutions to help people in organizations develop talented women. Many of the current books on women and leadership have as their focus the relevant research studies or essays from thought leaders in women's leadership. Their emphasis has been on delineating the results from academic and field research and offering commentary on the current state of women's leadership. While these have been invaluable to advancing the field of women's leadership to academics and researchers, they have not been an easy read for most people.

In contrast, this book will appeal to those working in organizations on the "front lines" every day and who have neither the inclination nor time to read a scholarly tome about leadership development. It is written for those whose split-second decisions have far-ranging influence on who gets promoted, on the climate created in their organization, and whether or not the company is perceived as a good place to work. This volume uniquely translates the findings from social science research into strategies and tips that people in management can apply.

Acknowledgments

Many people have helped me with this book and I thank them for their contributions. My deep gratitude goes to Debra Robinson and Robert J. Lee who helped me to refine my ideas, read the first drafts, and provided consistent support and encouragement throughout the entire process. I would like to thank Dick Kilburg for the seminal discussions that sparked this book and for providing his wisdom about the process of writing. Diana Cunningham's superb librarianship saved me countless hours that would have been spent in researching articles and refining the initial draft of the manuscript. Special thanks to Marian Ruderman and Martin Wilcox for their help in the development of the article that appeared in CCL's *Leadership in Action* publication.

I am especially grateful to the five high-achieving women who graciously consented to anonymously write the first-hand accounts that appear in Chapter 7. Your heartfelt stories breathe life and meaning into the research findings. Your lives and work inspire those who know you personally, and now your influence extends to the women and men who are touched by reading your narratives.

There were many people whose support and advice were invaluable, and I am thankful for their various contributions: Judith Albino, Elizabeth Barasch, Mariangela Battista, Victoria Berger-Gross, Traci Berliner, Sue A. Brush, Dianne Chong, Allan Church, Michelle Crosby, Lynne Doherty, Katharine Frase, Amy George, Nathalie Gingras, Andrea Goldberg, Shami Goswami, Dee Hall, Katherine

Hegmann, Christie Hicks, Nancy Hill, Ann Howard, Florence Hudson, Anita Jensen, Shauna King, Wendy Kornreich, Pamela M. Larrick, Marianne Lepre-Nolan, M. Ann Levett, Lisette Manzi, Cathy Martine, Nancy McKinstry, Carla Murray, Yvonne M. Perkins, Bill Schiemann, Elizabeth J. Smith, Gwendolyn Sykes, Lisa Tedesco, Michelle Tenzyk, Cindy Thompson, and Anne Weisberg. A special note of thanks to Laura Sabattini, Steve Temlock, and Marsha Temlock. In addition to those whom I can thank by name, I am also grateful to those who preferred not to have this public acknowledgement.

For their expertise in graphics design, I thank Michael Brennan Taylor and Allan G. Davis.

I am also grateful to the editorial team who brought this book to fruition: Steven Rogelberg for his thoughtful suggestions and leadership of the book series, Lise Saari for her early support on this project and for her insights and comments on the manuscript, and Christine Cardone for her expertise as Executive Editor, Wiley-Blackwell.

Writing a book requires a sustained effort over a period of time. I am very appreciative for the ongoing love and support of family members, Angela DiGioia, Anne and Jean Mauro, and Cindy Mauro Reisenauer.

Part I

Historical and Current Contexts for Women's Leadership

Chapter 1

Introduction

Women's leadership invites questions and requires answers. As you have been observing the changes occurring in the world today, many of you may be asking some of the following questions:

- Why aren't there more women leaders?
- What has happened to the numbers of women who have entered the workforce in the past thirty years?
- Why aren't more of them in senior leadership roles?
- Why have women been leaving organizations to become entrepreneurs?
- What is important for men to know about women's leadership and vice versa?
- What insights will enable men and women to work more effectively together?
- If there were more women leaders, would the world be a better place?
- How can men and women work together to co-create organizations that serve all stakeholders well?
- How can men and women use their combined strengths to arrive at creative solutions to meet the challenges facing the world?

It is clear that we must examine women's leadership in conjunction with that of men. This book is aimed at helping readers, especially employers, gain a deeper understanding of the gender-related issues that affect the behaviors of both women and men at work. It's aimed at women, men, their bosses, CEOs, Human Resource (HR) executives and professionals, coaches and their clients, and researchers.

We already know a fair amount about how to develop leaders. A large percentage of what we know about leadership development applies equally to women as to men. How can we use this knowledge to increase the pool of women leaders? Demographic changes are bringing shortages of talent. This book offers some practical suggestions to assist you in growing the leadership of people you care about, developing women successors, and building the pipeline of talent for your organization. This book is meant to be a practical guide, one that is grounded in research from the social sciences, particularly psychology. It will help you to make changes in jobs and workplaces that foster fairness, productivity, and innovation. Individual men and women cannot wait for organizations to change, and organizations cannot wait for society to change. It will require courage on the part of individual men and women to take on the task of assisting each other in co-creating organizations that will serve them well in the twenty-first century. Many of you who read this book are more than ready for the challenge. This book intends to "arm" you with knowledge, strategies, and skills to accelerate your efforts.

Demographic trends tell us that when the large number of so-called Baby Boomers in the United States begins to retire in the next several years, there will be an even greater shortage of trained, experienced people who can fill key positions. Because the smaller Generation X (born between 1965 and 1979) will serve as the replacement group, an urgent task for many organizations is to fill the pipeline of executive talent with individuals who are ready to move into leadership roles. With the challenges posed by the dearth of leadership, global organizations need to better understand how to develop talented people, regardless of gender, race, and ethnicity. For a variety of reasons, the attraction and retention of talented individuals, particularly women, have already become an important issue for many American corporations. Frustrated by what they view as limited options in a corporate setting, many women choose to leave large organizations. The retention of talented women in corporations has become even more critical in light of recent research by *Catalyst*[1] which shows that companies with large representations of women have better financial performance.

As a result of the increased awareness concerning the importance of leadership, it is time to examine the information from both practice and research to answer the questions:

• How do we best develop women leaders?
• What can men and women in organizations do to develop talented women?
• Are there leadership development approaches that are especially effective for women?
• What can managers and organizations do to develop talented women?

A strong case can be made that this book is overdue because of the growing recognition of the need for talent management in organizations, the growth of leadership development methodologies in the marketplace, and the demographic imperatives to develop talented women executives.

Isn't it a bit presumptuous, if not foolhardy, to expect that any changes can be wrought at the individual or organizational level when cultural and societal forces reinforce traditional gender role patterns? Well, we need to start somewhere. Rather than wait for things to change, you may want to be proactive in effecting change in whatever role or level you are now. Whatever your role in your organization, you may want to do whatever it takes. Depending on where you sit in an organization, you have the opportunity to change what you do every day as an individual contributor, local supervisor, divisional head, a member of the top leadership team, or the CEO. These changes may range from something as seemingly simple as selecting people to serve on a team to creating the policies and practices affecting the entire corporate body.

Even with the progress that has been made, women seeking leadership positions face persistent barriers to their success. These include gender bias in leadership opportunities, gender inequalities in family responsibilities, inflexibility in workplace structures, and inadequacies in social policies. The costs of the lack of diversity in leadership are borne by individual women and men, their families, the organizations that employ them, and, of course, by the society that permits the inequality to occur. Strategies for improvement are therefore required at the organizational, individual, and societal level – all of which are interdependent. This book hopes to give you some ideas and strategies for improvement at the individual and organizational levels; and, in so doing, also give you the courage to do what you can to move forward with change. In the future, more attention may be placed on changing the institutional and societal structures and policies to better enable the emergence of leaders who reflect the diversity of the society.

How This Book Is Organized

The book consists of three sections:

- Part I includes the Introduction and discusses the purpose of the book, its value at this point in time, and the pros and cons of addressing the issue of developing women's leadership as separate from leadership in general. This section sets the stage for understanding the relevance of developing women by providing a historical and a current context for it. Women's leadership is discussed in light of the driving forces for organizational change, relevant demographics related to generational trends in employment and educational attainment, and the current issues in the United States that impact everyone – not just women, such as: gender role expectations, dual careers, and work–life integration. This section also covers what is important to know about leadership and its development. It includes highlights from current research on leadership behaviors and an inventory of options for developing effective leaders
- Part II contains practical suggestions for organizations, managers, and women. It contains ideas for CEOs, HR executives, and their teams to implement in their organizations, using examples from some "best practice" companies. This section includes information on what male and female bosses can do to help develop women leaders, what women can do to develop themselves and other women leaders, and what organizations can do to retain and develop their talented women. Highlights will be presented from pertinent research results on the topic of gender and leadership. Comments from the author's interviews with executive women and men will be used to underscore research findings.
- Part III offers both a present and a future focus on women's leadership. It contains firsthand accounts from highly successful women

of their experience of becoming leaders. They tell their stories of how they managed to get where they are and accomplish what they do. Each woman leader speaks frankly and from the heart about some of her defining moments as a leader, the role played by mentors and others, and lessons learned. The advice that each one imparts to women will also – no surprise here – be relevant for men. A final chapter suggests future directions for women's leadership, particularly as it relates to the changing demographics of a global workforce. It also includes some potential topic areas for researchers to explore.

How to Use This Book Most Effectively

The discussions in each chapter are short, focused answers to those questions that summarize the pertinent research for that topic sprinkled with examples from the interviews I have been conducting with women and men on the topic of how best to develop women leaders. At the beginning of most chapters there is a list of the "Topics to be Covered in this Chapter" to enable you to see where the chapter is going and to provide an easy reference. Boxes labeled *Tips*, or *Examples*, or *Good to Know* provide user-friendly summaries followed by fuller explanations when necessary.

The book need not be read sequentially. You may choose to go directly to particular topics on an as-needed basis. Or, if you have a specific question about developing women leaders, you can go directly to the relevant chapter to obtain the information quickly.

If you want an overall understanding of the issues associated with developing women leaders, then you may wish to read the book straight through. Chapters 3 and 5 contain many valuable research findings that will provide you with the foundation for understanding the recommendations made throughout the book.

In summary, this book translates research-based best practices, ideas, and concepts into sensible, concrete actions to enable men and women to be more effective in developing women leaders.

Your Role in Developing Women's Leadership

Every organization has its own approach to talent management. Some organizations use all known available methodologies and have made leadership development a major focus of human resource strategy.

Other organizations have paid little attention to developing diverse slates of candidates for leadership roles and have paid the price in high turnover. It is my hope that, whatever your vantage point, whether as a woman seeking to advance her career, as a CEO of a company who wishes to set an example to others about how to foster diversity, as an HR professional with responsibility for talent management, or as a manager who now finds himself reporting to female bosses or with several female direct reports, this book will help to open up dialogues that can occur between male and female colleagues. Only by having a willingness to learn from each other, to try out new behaviors that may seem strange at first, and to persevere with the intent of working cooperatively together will we arrive at the collective wisdom necessary to create organizations that will enable our culture and economy to thrive. The rewards are many and include the possibility of new markets, products, and solutions that serve the worldwide community of women and men.

This book translates the relevant social science research into some ideas for best practices for men and women, managers and organizations. In so doing, this book offers sensible ideas that you can use every day in the workplace. With the understanding that there is no "one-size-fits-all" strategy, some of these ideas will be appropriate in some settings and not in others. You will need to judge for yourself and select the best strategies that are most likely to be effective for your circumstances.

As a device to help you think about your own individual situation and consider your strategies for effecting change, you may find it helpful to consider three "categories of gender issue concerns" in determining how and when to take action. Suggested for use expressly for the ideas in this volume, these three "categories of gender issue concerns" encompass *absolute*, *transitional*, and *fairness* concerns.

Absolute gender concerns deal with the absolute differences between the genders such as those involving motherhood and physical differences. For example, because females are the ones to nurse infants, there is an absolute or unconditional quality to such issues as whether or not to include lactation room facilities in building designs or renovations. The timeframe for these actions may be longer, that is, they may take more time for consideration or implementation.

Transitional concerns deal with moving from one state or condition to another and require you to focus on "transitioning" from the present state to a future one. Your actions may accelerate changes. For example, presently there are not enough women leaders as role models. In order to effect change, you are required to figure out how to increase the numbers of women in the pipeline, what actions to take to develop them, and the implications of the increase in numbers for the organization. Transitional concerns may change in the future provided that certain steps are taken in the present.

Fairness concerns deal with more immediate issues of equal opportunity and fairness and can be dealt with more directly or very quickly. This might include policies and practices surrounding equal employment opportunity (EEO) issues, intimacy in the workplace, or how to deal with people's misconceptions and subtle biases. For example, you may see that one of your managers tends to give lower performance ratings to women or avoids giving them the best jobs. You can have a discussion with that manager and monitor results in a short timeframe.

Because this book has a very practical focus for men and women in organizations, and before moving on, I want to note what this book does not attempt to do:

- This book does not try to present a totally comprehensive review of the literature on leadership in general, women's leadership, and gender differences.
- This book does not attempt to explain "how to" set up internal large-scale leadership development programs or to integrate mentoring, women's networks, or coaching with an established leadership development program.
- This book is not a cookbook with recipes of do's and don'ts. For example, there are no magic formulas for how to attract, recruit, or retain talented women. Rather, this book is meant to be a practical guide – grounded in research from the social sciences, particularly psychology – to help managers and organizations understand what processes and practices are likely to be successful in the development of talented women.

Chapter 2

Why Women's Leadership Today Invites Questions and Requires Answers

What is it about women's leadership that invites questions and requires answers? Whether you are a man or a woman, you are affected every day by decisions made by leaders in organizations. Due to history and culture, most of the decisions have been made by male leaders. Looking at the trends in the recent past and their impact on how you live your life can help you sharpen your perspective on the issues you face now.

Why pay attention to the development of women's leadership? Are there more similarities or differences in the way men and women lead others? If so, what can both genders learn from this information? How will having greater knowledge about leadership help both women and men create better organizations for their employees, customers, and shareholders? And personally, what can you do to make the most of *all* of your talented people? What actions can you take to enable women and men to grow in wisdom, developing into fine leaders whom others would want to follow? How can this book help you develop your own leadership?

These are some of the questions that will be answered throughout the chapters of this book. This chapter presents some historical highlights and the current context in which leadership development occurs for women. It sets the stage by taking a brief look at some of the critical factors that affect women's leadership including: recent social changes that have impacted the roles of men and women; the driving forces underlying organizational and social change;

generational demographics producing the need for talent management; women's advances in education and career attainment; and work–life integration. It will also provide a lens to help you interpret the changes we are all witnessing as we move into this twenty-first century. Is women's leadership "for women only"? Definitely not!

Topics covered in this chapter include:

- Definition of Leadership
- Key Historical Events and Present Realities
- Driving Forces behind Organizational Change
- Women's Achievements: Educational Attainment and in the Workforce
- Women Leaders Are Good for Business
- Generations in the Workforce
- Work–Life Integration

Good to Know:
How Is Leadership Defined?

Leadership has been defined in many ways, but the working definition used in this book is a very broad one: a leader is a person who influences and directs the behaviors of others. Leadership can be conferred formally or informally, and consists of: motivating, inspiring, persuading, and exercising authority. In general, leaders enable groups of people to achieve shared goals. In this discussion, the terms *leader* and *manager* will be used interchangeably and will refer to leadership in all types of organizations, companies, cities, and countries.

Recent History

To say that in the past four decades (1970–2010) there has been tremendous social change in the United States is an understatement. Women today have achieved educational levels and entered the workforce in numbers that were unthinkable fifty years ago. Women are now an economic force with buying power of their own. But women's advancement into leadership roles has been an evolution, not a revolution. As I tell my clients in Fortune 500 companies, women are relative newcomers on the corporate scene. They are still forging new ground as pioneers in this landscape. The challenge associated with maintaining the dual roles as leaders and mothers is a relatively recent phenomenon affecting increasing numbers of women in organizations over the past twenty years. More recently, as the younger generations of males become more involved in child-rearing, many men struggle, too, to integrate their roles as fathers and leaders. Child care is no longer just "women's work," and many men want to be more involved, spending time with their families. More and more of them are "Mr. Mom." So it is important to take a historical look at some twentieth-century societal changes in order to develop a perspective of how men's and women's roles have been converging and what these changes suggest for the present and future workforce.

Key Historical Events from the 1920s to the 1960s

Changes in legislation and technology brought about many profound changes in the status of women in the twentieth century. Moving from an agricultural economy to an industrial economy meant that fewer people made their living on farms, and more were employed in industrial urban areas. It also meant a weakening of the traditional division of labor in which males did the heavy, physical labor required on farms, and women performed the domestic tasks involved with cooking, cleaning, laundry, and child-rearing, often for families consisting of five or more children. An increase in office jobs meant that there were fewer jobs that required physical strength, and more that required strong cognitive and verbal abilities, job tasks that could be performed by women. In 1925, the percentage of women in the labor force was approximately 20%. This percentage has risen steadily ever since, despite The Great Depression of the 1930s and the ensuing baby boom which continued until 1964.

During the World War II years (1939–45), the available workforce at home contained larger numbers of women, and it became clear that women's abilities led them to perform jobs that had previously been done by men. Examples include the roles portrayed by the familiar icon "Rosie the Riveter," as well as the cadre of female pilots who expertly ferried complex and sophisticated airplanes across the United States – a vital but often overlooked contribution toward winning the war. When the war was over, many of the women who had worked in factories and offices and flown those planes got married and had children, and, unless they needed to work for economic reasons, the gender role expectation was that they go back to being homemakers. Even into the 1960s, although it was acceptable for married women to work, the gender role expectation was that women with children would stop working during pregnancy and stay home to raise children.

The knowledge-based and service economy grew relatively rapidly. By the mid-1960s, the participation of women in the labor force reached 40%. At this time, female roles continued to emphasize the professions of teaching, nursing, and social work. The majority of women were in individual contributor, non-managerial, and support roles as secretary, nurse, teacher, librarian, social worker. It was during the 1960s, however, that technological progress brought greater control over reproduction through the use of "the pill" as a contraceptive method. The number of children in families could be planned and reduced, and women entered the workforce in greater numbers.

Another watershed event occurred in the 1960s: the passage of civil rights legislation. The 1963 Equal Pay Act and Title VII of the 1964 Civil Rights Act made discrimination in employment unlawful on the basis of sex, race, color, religion, and national origin. Title VII prohibits disparate treatment of applicants and employees, defined as treating workers differently based on their membership in a protected class.

Present Realities

Despite this landmark federal legislation, the many cases brought before the courts in the more than forty years since its enactment cannot eliminate the subtle forms of discrimination which are difficult to prove or address in the legal system. Ironically, the catch to these protections has been that existing employment laws are based on principles of equal treatment and are written to be gender neutral. The assumption is that men and women have equal and similar situations and should be treated the same. But men and women are not "similarly situated": the prime example is the "situation" of pregnancy and motherhood. As a result, gender-neutral laws designed for equal protection may not necessarily produce gender-equal outcomes in most employment settings.[1] Even after adjusting for all the ways in which men's and women's participation in the workforce differ, in 2007 women earned median weekly wages of 80 cents for every dollar earned by men.[2] The effects of this pay differential cannot be underestimated. The subtle "psychological put-down" it conveys can take its toll on women in the workplace, both individually and collectively. It has also been a major factor contributing to the high turnover and the exodus of women from large organizations. Much has been written in the public press about the numbers of talented women starting their own businesses, where their entrepreneurship allows them flexibility and freedom.

Subtle discrimination typically occurs through preferences and biases which nearly everyone has, but of which we are largely unaware. More will be said later about how these preferences and prejudices influence our stereotypes about men and women and how this leads us to draw faulty conclusions about people's competencies and their performance as leaders. These unconscious considerations are especially important because pay is awarded on the basis of performance evaluations.

The harsh reality remains and there is still gender inequality in pay. That women are underpaid for similar work is now a truism in the United States. The wage gap needs to be eliminated, because fundamentally it is unfair, and because, in the long run, it disadvantages so many.

Metaphors through Time: From Concrete Wall to Glass Ceiling to Labyrinth

In their comprehensive book about the challenges facing women as they strive to be leaders, *Through the Labyrinth*, authors Alice Eagly and Linda Carli discuss three barriers that have obstructed women's advancement: the concrete wall, the glass ceiling, and the labyrinth. The "concrete wall" existed in an era when there were separate and distinct gender roles: men were breadwinners and women were homemakers. Although women gained the right to vote in 1920, they still faced many barriers to leadership. Access to most of the Ivy

League universities, credentials that historically opened doors to leadership positions for males, was denied until the 1960s. In the early 1970s women were routinely discouraged from learning the "trades" such as plumber, electrician, or carpenter; and women faced hostile environments in such occupations as firefighter and construction worker. In the business world, even women with college degrees were channeled into clerical and bank teller positions, with typing as a requisite and relatively low pay.

The concrete wall began to crumble in the 1970s and by the mid-1980s women were employed in middle management jobs but faced an invisible barrier that excluded them from the upper levels of management. Women were described as bumping into the "glass ceiling,"[3] that imperceptible impediment that nevertheless restricted access to higher-level jobs and pay. In many organizations, bright and talented women would get promoted to a particular level, and then found that only one or two made it beyond that point. An underlying attitude that contributed to the existence of the "glass ceiling" was the notion that it was too risky to employ women, because they would quit their jobs to raise a family. As the situation has evolved, more women have surmounted the obstacles and found the paths to the top of organizations. Eagly and Carli have labeled these circuitous paths a "labyrinth" that contains numerous barriers, albeit not as obvious as they were in the past. Differences in gender roles still require that women spend more time in the caretaking of loved ones and in the management and performance of household tasks. The labyrinth metaphor is another depiction of the situation facing today's women as they make their way through the twists and turns and hurdles of the organizational maze to achieve power, authority, wealth, and prestige.

Driving Forces behind Organizational Change

For the past four decades, there have been many changes in the world of work. Post World War II corporations were modeled on a hierarchical, military model of leadership, and a top-down, "command and control" approach to decisions was taken by those who had risen to executive levels in organizations. This top-down style of leadership in which decision making was in the hands of a few leaders at the top of an organization was prevalent through the 1980s, when the WWII generation still occupied positions of power in organizations. But there have been driving forces and technological advances since the 1990s that have brought momentous changes to the way in which work is performed in organizations. Some of these driving forces are listed in the box below.

Driving Forces behind Changes in the Workplace from the 1990s to the Present[4]

- Globalization of business, extending to vendors, resources, markets, and competition
- Focus on e-business and a reliance on technology that can deliver information instantly
- A fiercely competitive marketplace, with its premium on speed, savvy, and flexibility
- Greater integration of the world economy and its attendant knowledge requirements
- Dissemination of information about the environmental issues that affect our planet, such as trends in global warming and supplies of natural resources such as oil, coal, and water
- More teamwork and greater emphasis on lateral rather than vertical relationships
- Flatter, leaner, more empowered workforces charged with making rapid decisions
- Increasing pressure to produce short-term financial results
- The proliferation of alliances, acquisitions, partnerships, and joint ventures
- The rapid growth of emerging markets in India, China, and other parts of the world
- Shifts in values and priorities associated with younger generations, dual-career marriages, and domestic responsibilities
- Different generations in the workforce

These driving forces for change have placed new demands on the entire workforce and particularly on those who serve in leadership roles. Work demands placed on leaders related to global relationships and travel, business complexity, and faster organizational change have increased. Workforces are located around the globe, and bosses have a harder time developing or even *knowing* their direct reports! Telephone calls with coworkers located across the globe extend the workday into the late evening or early morning in order to find the optimal time to accommodate the majority on a work team.

The pace of change has accelerated and a premium is placed on speed. As *New York Times* columnist and Pulitzer Prize-winning author Thomas L. Friedman argues, we live in a global information economy.[5] The flow of information is flattening and shrinking the world in its wake and is bringing together more and more individuals from the far-flung reaches of the globe. This globalization is being driven by groups of individuals who are more diverse – in gender and ethnicity.

As both line managers and human resource professionals have known for the past several years, talent management has become the number one issue facing many organizations. As the trend toward globalization implies, there is a strong need to optimize the talents of both domestic and international multi-cultural workforces.

With the retirement of large numbers of Baby Boomers (born 1946–64), and the smaller numbers of Generation X (born 1965–79) to provide replacements, the need exists for a well-qualified cadre of executives ready to step into leadership roles. Under these circumstances, diversity becomes critical. With fewer people available for the workforce, the pool of potential leaders could be insufficient unless it draws on women and all races and ethnicities.

More Women in the Workforce than Ever Before

The numbers of women in the workforce continue to grow. In 1988, the shares of labor force participation were 45% for women and 55% for men. In 2008, women now make up 48% of the workforce (including both full-time and part-time workers).[6] According to the U.S. Bureau of Labor Statistics, labor force participation rates will continue to rise for women.

Women's Educational Attainment

Women now attain more education than men. What do the numbers tell us about the educational qualifications of future job candidates?

Beginning in 1950, the percentage of Bachelor's degrees awarded to women began to rise, and in 1981–82 actually surpassed the 50% mark. According to a July 9, 2006 *New York Times* article, "At Colleges, Women are Leaving Men in the Dust," "Women now make up 58 percent of those enrolled in two- and four-year colleges; and are, over all, the majority in graduate schools and professional schools, too."[7] According to 2008–09 projections from the U.S. National Center for Education Statistics, women earn 59% of the Bachelor's degrees, 61% of Master's degrees and 49% of Ph.Ds; this upward trend continues into the future.[8]

Women as Corporate Officers: The Current Situation

Although women's visibility in leadership roles has grown, the numbers tell the true story. What are the numbers? *Fortune* magazine (15 October 2007 issue on "The 50 Most Powerful Women") reported that for publicly held companies, there are thirteen women who are CEOs with sixteen more on the international list. According to *Catalyst*, an organization founded to promote the advancement of women in business and the professions, its 2005 *Census of Women Corporate Officers and Top Earners of the Fortune 500* revealed that women held 16.4% of 10,873 corporate officer positions (defined as corporate executives who were board-elected or board-appointed), which was only 0.7 percentage points more than in 2002. These results indicate that in three years, growth in the percentage of corporate officer positions held by women slowed dramatically. At this estimated growth rate for the past ten years, it will take forty years for women to reach parity with men in corporate officer ranks. Comparison of line and staff roles also showed a great deal of gender segregation. Corporate officers in line positions, considered to have greater clout, are responsible for an organization's profits and losses, while those in staff positions support the auxiliary functioning of the business. Women held only 10.6% of corporate officer line positions, while men held 89.4% of line positions. Women had greater percentages of corporate officer positions in industries where women were 49% or more of the total workforce, such as finance, insurance, real estate, retail trade, and services.

Women Leaders Are a Driving Force for Powering Business

As the demographics of the U.S. marketplace and employee base are shifting, it makes sense for companies to expand their leadership to include people who reflect the gender composition of the marketplace and can relate to the issues faced by customers, employees, suppliers, and shareholders. Using mathematical modeling and case studies to show how variety in staffing produces organizational strength,[9] researcher Scott Page notes: "There's a lot of empirical data to show that diverse cities are more productive, diverse boards of directors make better decisions, the most innovative companies are diverse."

Are women leaders good for business? The answer is: yes. As U.S. businesses expand into new markets, cultures, and workforces across the United States and around the world, the companies that integrate gender diversity into their business strategy prove to be more successful. The 2004 *Catalyst* study, "The Bottom Line: Connecting Corporate Performance and Gender Diversity," has shown that the Fortune 500 companies with the highest percentages of women corporate officers experienced, on average, a 35.1% higher return on equity (ROE) and 34.0% higher total return to shareholders (TRS) than did those with the lowest percentage of women corporate officers. Although this does not prove causation, it shows a strong correlation between companies that have diversified their senior management and companies that performed well financially. As Figure 2.1 illustrates, the presence of women leaders in an organization may be likened to a central gearwheel, which meshes with others and serves as a driving force for powering the engines of business success.

Generations in the Workforce

There have been shifts in values and priorities associated with the work and home life of younger generations, dual-career marriages, and the 24/7 nature of work. Much has been written in the media about the controversial differences between the Baby Boomers, Gen X, and Gen Y. Definitions of the generations are given in the box below.

Definitions:
How are the generations defined?[10]

In the 2005 brief by the Families and Work Institute, "Generation and Gender in the Workplace," the generations were defined as follows:

Generation	Years of Birth
Baby Boomers	1946 through 1964
Gen X	1965 through 1979
Gen Y	starting in 1980

The Gen X and Gen Y employees are increasingly the children of working mothers and the children of the downsized generation.

Figure 2.1 Women leaders are a driving force for powering business

Gen X and Gen Y individuals are more likely to be family-centric or dual-centric, that is, placing a higher priority on family or on work and family equally. Interestingly, employees who are dual-centric or family-centric exhibit greater satisfaction with their lives, and report higher levels of job satisfaction than employees who are work-centric. Research published in 2005 by the Families and Work Institute, "Generation and Gender in the Workplace," has shown that Gen X fathers perform more childcare than Baby Boomer fathers, and Gen Y fathers perform more than all.[11] It is now a common sight to see men pushing baby strollers or as the sole adult playing with their children in public parks.

Despite these occurrences, women still perform more of the tasks that need to be done frequently, or even daily, such as cooking, cleaning, and laundry, rather than those performed intermittently, such as home repairs, car maintenance, or outdoor work. Women are more likely to be the home managers, keeping track of children's scheduled activities involving school events and extracurricular activities such as piano lessons and soccer practice. As one female general manager at a large, high-tech company noted: "Because most males don't have the responsibility for household duties, they don't understand the challenges that household duties represent. Many men just don't think about it." As home managers they also perform the monitoring function, reminding spouses of events in the daily schedule and keeping track of birthdays, anniversaries, etc., for the extended family.

It is females and not males who are still socialized to maintain the relationships among family and friends, to be the "glue" that connects people. Some of the requirements associated with this "social director" role are arranging events involving family celebrations, serving as the main point of contact for teachers and school administrators, chauffeuring and making arrangements for children's activities, communicating via telephone or email with extended family members and neighbors, and even hand-writing the occasional "thank-you" note. All of these functions can serve to keep families intact and create support systems that contribute to the psychological health and overall well-being of the family members.

As stated in a front-page *New York Times Magazine* article (15 June 2008), by Lisa Belkin, "In a family where Mom stays home and Dad goes to work, she spends 15 hours a week caring for children and he spends 2. In families in which both parents are wage earners, Mom's average drops to 11 and Dad's goes up to 3. Lest you think this is a significant improvement over our parents and grandparents, not so fast ... none of this is all that different, in terms of ratio, from 90 years ago."[12]

Work–life Integration – Shared by Both Genders

Historically, women's responsibilities for domestic care (housework, childcare, eldercare) have been far greater than men's. Although the father's time with children has increased, for every hour of childcare done by men, women do more than double that amount (2.1 hours). Married women with children are more likely than their husbands to work "two shifts,"[13] one at their paid job and one at home. Adding to the pressure is the trend to spend more quality time with children. The challenges faced by many female executives with children, therefore, are greater than those of their male counterparts who may have wives who do not work outside the home. It can slow them down as they move through career tracks, or even sideline them completely when faced with the challenges of taking care of the needs of children or elders.

With the greater prevalence of dual-career marriages among younger generations, however, men increasingly share domestic responsibilities for housework and childcare. In the words of one interviewee in a dual-career marriage: "Those early morning meetings at 7:00 a.m. really impact family time. When these are not emergency meetings, you really have to question if it is necessary to hold them at that hour of the morning. No one gets to be home with the kids, getting them ready for school." As men become more engaged in family work, they express a greater desire for more reasonable hours, resist demands for unscheduled, overtime work, and express the wish to take time off for child-related reasons – behaviors that have traditionally been associated with female employees. As the *NY Times* article stated, "Gender should not determine the division of labor at home. It's a message consistent with nearly every major social trend of the past three decades – women entering the workforce, equality between the sexes, the need for two incomes to pay the bills, even courts that favor shared custody after divorce."[14] It is clear that work–life integration is no longer in the realm of women's issues but is one that is now shared by men, women, and their families. It reaches beyond individuals, Human Resources departments, and organizations toward a set of social issues that, as we will see later in Chapter 4, are relevant to sustainable business success on a national and global level.

Summary

In summary, we have looked at some key events in the evolution of women's achievement in the United States and the impact of legislation and technology. Women are now achieving levels of education that are unparalleled in our history and that now surpass those of men. Organizations are experiencing a need for a qualified cadre of talented individuals ready to assume leadership roles. When faced with many of the challenges of functioning in the business world, a domain that, in the past, has been populated mostly by males, many women may be tempted to give up their dreams of achievement. In so doing, they forfeit the creativity and perspective that they bring to an organization or a cause, and deny themselves the satisfaction, the rewards, and the self-confidence that can come from making significant contributions to an enterprise. What is equally unfortunate is the price that organizations pay when they are deprived of the contributions of 51% of the world's population. The driving forces behind change in today's workplace pose challenges to both men and women, as they struggle to give their lives purpose and meaning. What might organizations and the people in them do to address these challenges? What solutions may be applied that enable positive outcomes for individuals, families, societies, and the economy as a whole? What might you *personally* do? In the next chapters you will learn what actions you can take to meet these challenges.

Chapter 3

What Women and Men Need to Know About Leadership and Its Development

What makes a leader effective? What do we know about the behavior of successful leaders? Plenty! Thanks, in part, to the bad behavior of corporate leaders in the 1990s! Scandals involving Enron, Tyco, WorldCom, and others resulted in a renewed focus on understanding the components of good leadership. Why is it crucial to understand the factors that affect leadership? Because the lessons of history remind us that the consequences of bad leadership, whether for an organization or a government, can be so calamitous that they can affect the well-being and the economic health of masses of people over decades and whole lifetimes. Stated more positively, in an increasingly diverse, complex world, our understanding of those factors can help us grow the pools of talented people and prepare them to be tomorrow's leaders.

Although writing and theorizing about leadership has been around for centuries, modern organizations and contemporary management science have defined leadership in ways that enable us to use some language to introduce ideas and communicate with each other. In this chapter we will be shining a spotlight on what we know about some state-of-the-art scientific and practical approaches to leadership. As you read about these concepts, kindly remember that no one book or chapter can do justice to the different approaches that have emerged from the attempts to understand what constitutes good leadership.

This chapter distills a vast amount of material on leadership research and practice into some solid key points for you to know to take actions appropriate for your needs and circumstances.

Questions you may have about leadership and its development are:

- What does leadership research reveal about the behaviors of effective leaders?
- What, if any, are the gender differences in leadership?
- How important are leadership development practices such as challenging job assignments, coaching, mentoring, and development programs?
- Of what special significance is their application to the development of talented women?

Topics covered in this chapter include the following:

- Leadership Research
  - Leadership Competencies
  - Personality Traits
  - Leadership Styles
  - Transformational and Transactional Leadership
- Leadership Practices
  - Challenging Job Assignments
  - Coaching
  - Mentoring
  - Development Programs

What Does Leadership Research Reveal About the Behavior of Effective Leaders?

Being successful as a leader in today's organizations is a complex and difficult task! Women and men in leadership roles or who aspire to become leaders in their organizations may want to better understand the many factors involved in the emergence of leadership. These factors include: leadership competencies necessary for success, attitudes about male and female managers, intelligence, personality, ethics, and leadership style.

Leadership Competencies

For the past couple of decades, organizations have found it useful to organize and describe the requirements for managerial and executive positions into competency models. Competency models contain lists of dimensions that are broader than skills and create a common language and blueprint for the behaviors that are expected of successful leaders.[1] Also sometimes called "leadership models" or "leadership competencies," they have become a feature in the human resource processes of best practice companies and may form the foundation for entire human resource systems including selection

---

Generic Senior Management Competency Model

Cognitive Abilities

- Judgment/Dealing with ambiguity
- Analyzing information/developing strategy
- Visionary thinking
- Global perspective

Interpersonal Skills

- Influencing, negotiating, managing conflict
- Building and sustaining relationships
- Collaborating with others

Communication Skills

- Listening to others
- Delivering presentations with impact

Leadership Abilities

- Motivating and inspiring others
- Drive for stakeholder success
- Managing execution
- Coaching and developing others
- Empowering individuals and teams

Technical Skills

- Demonstrating functional expertise
- Knowing the business
- Demonstrating industry knowledge
- Showing business acumen

and assessment, development, performance management and training. Competency models are usually considered to be proprietary information. An example of a generic senior management leadership competency model is shown in the box on the previous page.

Most competency models contain richer, more elaborate descriptions of the core abilities and skills shown in this simplified model in the box. A good competency model is tailored to the organizational culture.

Why Use Leadership Competencies?

An advantage for organizations that utilize competency models is that women and men learn what behaviors are effective to become strong leaders within that organization. When used in conjunction with rating scales, the competency models offer a way of evaluating both oneself and other managers with greater objectivity. Thus, training on the proper use of leadership competencies can assist people in making more objective judgments related to success or failure in a managerial role.

Why is objectivity so important and what does it have to do with gender, leadership, and bias? Well, apparently we need all the help we can get when it comes to growing diverse talent in our organizations. Extensive evidence from large-scale studies of gender differences shows that males and females are alike on most (but not all) psychological variables, such as cognitive abilities, verbal and nonverbal communication, and personality variables, to name a few.[2]

Despite the fact that women and men show more similarities than differences, gender stereotypes can narrow the range of behaviors we accept from men and women. Results from research studies that span more than three decades have shown that people usually rate managers as showing more stereotypical traits similar to men than to women. In what researchers term the "think manager – think male" mindset, leaders, in general, are viewed as possessing more masculine characteristics than feminine characteristics.[3] Traditional gender stereotypes depict women as deficient in the attributes believed necessary to succeed as a manager. Furthermore, in ratings made by male managers, women managers were characterized as less rational in their approach to the world than were men.[4] When this attitude is not held in check or adjusted by facts, a manager with this opinion may continue to operate with blinders on by favoring a male candidate over a female candidate for the same position.

This erroneous way of thinking can have serious consequences for managers and organizations. It can foster bias against women in managerial selection, placement, promotion, and training decisions. It also limits the range of behaviors that all leaders, both male and female, think of as acceptable for them to demonstrate. As you will see later in this chapter, the research on transformational leadership shows that women are very effective leaders. It makes sense, then, for leaders and organizations to understand the competencies, personality traits, and leadership styles that are most effective in today's marketplace.

Personality Traits Associated with Leadership

We know that general intelligence is one attribute that enhances job performance and occupational attainment in general.[5] However, intelligence alone does not account for the success of leaders. Certain personality traits improve one's chances for leadership.[6] Which ones are they? From administering carefully designed and validated personality tests to large numbers of people, researchers have organized personality attributes into five traits, known as the *Big Five*.[7] These *Big Five Personality Traits* are summarized in the box below.

Good to Know:
The Big Five Personality Traits

1. Openness to Experience: divergent thinking, flexibility, creativity, and resourcefulness.
2. Conscientiousness: strong work ethic, dependability, and self-discipline.
3. Extraversion: assertiveness, optimism, and sociability.
4. Agreeableness: trusting, altruistic, caring, and gentle qualities.
5. Neuroticism: showing emotional distress and negative emotions such as fear and anger.

What are the implications of these Big Five personality traits for leadership? People who demonstrate conscientiousness and extraversion are more likely to emerge as leaders. Effective leaders also show greater openness to experience, creativity, resourcefulness and can imagine the future of an organization. Agreeableness and Neuroticism are less important than the other personality traits in understanding leadership.[8] Leaders are often extraverts who tend to have an optimistic view of the future and are likely to inspire confidence and enthusiasm among followers. Successful leaders find ways of interacting with others, have wide networks of associates, build teams and motivate others. Leaders must also be willing to be open to new experiences, "think outside the box", take some risks, and be creative under uncertain conditions. Conscientious leaders, that is, those who are dependable and persistent, are more likely to plan for the monitoring and follow-up that are necessary to seeing a project to a successful conclusion.

What does the research on intelligence and personality show about the difference between men and women on these leadership qualities? Men and women differ little in general intelligence and in leadership abilities. Similarly, on the Big Five traits that are related to leadership – Extraversion, Openness to Experience, and Conscientiousness – men and women exhibit an overall gender balance. Extraversion exists at approximately the same level in men and women, although some differences are seen in some of the components of Extraversion. Extraversion consists of the following components: warmth, positive emotions, gregariousness, activity, assertiveness, and excitement seeking. Where are the differences? Women show greater warmth, sociability and positive emotions than men, and men demonstrate more assertiveness and excitement seeking than women.[9,10] Regarding the traits of Openness to Experience and Conscientiousness, there are mixed patterns of gender differences in their components. What do these gender differences suggest about actions to take? They suggest that the pattern of gender differences requires *both* men and women to attend to their development as leaders. No one gender has everything it takes to excel at leadership.

Might there be something to be gained by men and women, managers and organizations, by recognizing and acting on some of these differences? For example, what are the advantages for men and women leaders to "stretch" themselves by learning how to demonstrate some of the opposite-gender behaviors? Clearly, the outcomes of some managerial situations would be improved if it were more acceptable for female leaders to show more assertiveness and for male leaders to show more caring and empathy. To be effective, all leaders must examine their own strengths and challenge areas and determine what is needed for their own development. Some of the important questions that women and men need to raise about how leaders grow and develop are discussed later in this chapter.

Ethics

In addition to the Big Five, another quality with relevance for leadership is ethics. Ethical violations in corporations in recent years have resulted in inestimable losses to shareholders, employees, and the American public in general. As Eagly and Carli point out in their book, *Through the Labyrinth*,[11] the research shows some gender differences in ethics and morality. Among the whistle-blowers who have exposed recent major ethical violations in corporations, women are prevalent. Although gender differences in moral orientation are small, women, more than men, disapprove of unethical business practices such as lying, deceitful negotiations, bribery, and use of insider information. Men are more likely than women to engage in criminal activity. On tests used for personnel selection, women show greater self-reported integrity.

Every new breach of ethics that hits the news arouses concerns about morals in business and politics. Clearly, more research relating specific ethical qualities to leadership needs to be done. With an increased focus on ethics in business and government, questions to be asked are:

- Do these gender differences in ethics give women an advantage as leaders?
- By including more women in top management, can an organization decrease the occurrence of ethical violations and fraud?
- What might be the effects of increasing the numbers of women on boards of directors and top leadership teams?
- How might the existence of several women on a single team influence procedures and systems of "checks and balances" that could serve to prevent issues from escalating out of control?
- As nations increase the proportions of women in parliaments and governing bodies, will we see less corruption in governments?

Good to Know:
Leadership Styles[12]

- **Directive.** This style was formerly called *Autocratic* and entails command-and-control behavior that at times becomes coercive. It is most effective in crises but it eventually stifles creativity and initiative. Over the long term, it can lead to rebellion or passive resistance by employees.
- **Visionary.** When using this style, the leader gains employees' support by expressing responsibilities in the context of the organization's overall direction and strategy. It makes goals clear, increases employee commitment, and energizes a team. It is most effective when a new vision or direction is needed or when the manager is perceived as an expert. It is least effective when the manager is not perceived as credible or when trying to promote self-managed work teams.
- **Affiliative.** Leaders using this style emphasize maintaining relationships between and with employees, and their emotional needs over the job. It is most effective in getting diverse groups of individuals to work together harmoniously and when used in combination with visionary, participative, or coaching styles. It is least effective in crises or complex situations needing clear direction and control or when corrective performance

feedback is necessary for employees' improvement.
- **Participative.** Formerly called *Democratic*, this style is collaborative and democratic. Leaders using this style engage others, build consensus, and foster teamwork and participation in others. It is most effective when employees have at least as much information and knowledge as the manager. It is least effective in crises or when employees are incompetent or lack crucial information.
- **Pacesetting.** This style involves leading by example ("setting the pace") and personal heroics. Leaders using this style have high standards and tend to do much of the work themselves. Over time, this can discourage employees and can lead to the leader's burnout. It is most effective when quick results are required. It is least effective when employees need direction and development.
- **Coaching.** Leaders using this style are concerned with the long-term professional development and mentoring of employees. This style is appropriate in most managerial situations and should be part of any leader's repertoire. It is most effective when employees are motivated to take initiative and seek professional development. It is least effective in crises or when the manager lacks expertise.

Leadership Styles

In their roles as leaders, women and men must engage in activities to plan, organize, motivate, and control. In the execution of these activities, leaders must listen, set standards, develop action plans, give feedback, direct the actions of others, reward and punish, and develop employees. The extent to which leaders tend to demonstrate these different behaviors fall into patterns called "leadership styles." Leadership styles are a function of personal characteristics such as personality and values, the leadership styles the leader has observed in bosses, mentors, and other managers, the organization's values concerning "the right way" to manage, and the specific management situations faced by the leader. Spreier, Fontaine, & Malloy have identified six styles of leadership that managers use to motivate, reward, direct, and develop others.[13] Outstanding male and female leaders tend to demonstrate all styles in their behavioral repertoire and can vary their style according to the task, people, and situation to be managed. These leadership styles are summarized in the box.

Can one learn how to use different styles? Yes, and there are two key learning points here: 1) it is important to realize that there is not one right or wrong style – that the effectiveness of a style is, in fact, dependent on the management situation. More effective leaders demonstrate the ability to use the full repertoire of leadership styles, depending upon the managerial situation; and 2) the behaviors associated with each of the styles *can* be learned, despite one's preferences for certain styles over others.

What is important for men and women to know about leadership styles? Researchers have found that there is a tendency for women to adopt a more democratic (*Participative*) style and for men to adopt a more autocratic (*Directive*) style.[14] The give-and-take of collaborative decision making requires strong interpersonal skills and the ability to maintain good relationships despite having differing views with direct reports, peers, and others in the organization. It may be the case that taking charge in an autocratic, authoritative, assertive manner may lead to greater resistance toward female leaders than toward male leaders. On the other hand, male leaders, though freer to be more directive and autocratic, may find this style increasingly less appropriate in today's more team-based and less hierarchical organizations. More recently, as Eagly and Carli point out in their book, *Through the Labyrinth,* the research on *transformational* and *transactional leadership* has shown that there are some gender differences in leadership styles that have implications for both male and female leaders.

Transformational[15] and Transactional Leadership

In the past twenty years, there has been a shift in managerial styles away from a command-and-control type of leadership towards one marked by influence and collaboration. This shift emphasized that effective leaders inspire and motivate followers and nurture their development as individual contributors to the organization. Incorporating some of the concepts associated with the visionary, participative and coaching style, *Transformational* Leadership involves establishing oneself as a leader by communicating future goals and plans and by coaching and mentoring followers, thereby motivating them to contribute more effectively to their organization. *Transactional* Leadership, while also effective, involves managing in a more conventional way by monitoring employees, administering rewards for performance, and taking corrective actions for failures to meet goals. Most leaders utilize some combination of both control and influence strategies. A third style, called a *laissez-faire* style, is characterized by a lack of involvement and an avoidance of leadership responsibilities.

Women as Transformational Leaders

Researchers have assessed all of these styles by obtaining ratings of leaders and analyzing large-scale studies from thousands of managers. The results of these studies have found higher effectiveness overall for transformational leaders.[16] How do male and female managers compare on these leadership styles? Female leaders are more likely to be transformational leaders than male leaders.[17] Women leaders demonstrate more transformational leadership, particularly for those behaviors that communicate the organization's mission, examine new perspectives for solving problems, and develop and mentor followers. These closely resemble the *visionary, participative,* and *coaching styles* previously mentioned. Among the behaviors comprising transactional leadership, female leaders encourage others by providing rewards for satisfactory performance by followers.

In contrast, male leaders were more transactional than female leaders in "management-by-exception," that is, attending to followers' mistakes and waiting until problems become severe before intervening. Men, more than women, tend to avoid solving problems until they become more acute. In addition, men were more likely than women to be laissez-faire leaders, who are absent and uninvolved at critical junctures.

In summary, what do these results tell us about women leaders? Quite simply, women make excellent leaders. Women leaders are more likely to be visionary leaders, communicating future goals and plans to others. Blending participative and democratic behaviors into their repertoire, women leaders are more likely to provide attention and mentoring to develop subordinates. Women, more than men, use rewards to encourage and reinforce appropriate behaviors. For years, leadership researchers have urged managers to adopt more transformational styles to manage today's global organizations. Clearly, women are demonstrating the behaviors that are well suited to the task.

Now that we have answered some questions about effective leadership behaviors in the form of competencies, personality traits, and leadership styles, the next portion of this chapter is devoted to exploring some practices found to be successful in the development of leadership.

What Are Some Effective Leadership Development Practices?

As described in Chapter 2, the driving forces for organizational change have created seismic shifts in the structure of work. As organizations now regularly downsize, outsource, and flatten, people have learned to adjust to change and transition. The thirty-year career within one organization now occurs rarely, and one wonders if it is on its way to extinction. At one time, given the slower pace of business, organizations could take twenty years to develop someone for a vice president role. Now the time to develop most leaders has been compressed into a fraction of that time. People expect to be employed by numerous organizations during the course of their careers, necessitating repeated transitions and job assignments. Women and men report that they learn best through challenging job assignments.

Organizations can augment and accelerate their learning by using coaching, mentoring, and development programs.

Challenging Job Assignments

What are they? Challenging job assignments are job experiences that stretch people out of their comfort zone to do something new or different. These assignments are full of problems to solve, obstacles to overcome, and choices filled with risk and uncertainty. A new assignment can be an entirely new job or it can mean responsibilities added to an existing job. It need not be "assigned" to you, and in fact, you may wish to seek out and volunteer for these assignments because

---

Good to Know:
Definitions and Examples of Challenging Job Assignments[18]

Job Transitions

Take on new and broader responsibilities when old routines are inadequate.

- Making a lateral move to a different department
- Managing a group you know little about

Creating Change

Make strategic changes, fix preexisting problems, resolve poor performance issues.

- Launching a new product, project or system
- Reorganizing a business unit

High Levels of Responsibility

Meet clear deadlines, be visible to senior leaders so that success or failure is public.

- Managing large multiple functions, products, groups, or services
- Managing across geographic functions and tight deadlines

Managing Boundaries

Work with people over whom you have no formal authority.

- Influencing peers, senior management, external customers, unions, government
- Serving on a cross-functional team

Dealing with Diversity

Work across cultures, countries.

- Managing a diverse work group of people with gender, racial, ethnic, or religious backgrounds different from your own
- Taking an assignment in another country

---

they give you the opportunity to learn a great deal. How you respond to challenges – how you make decisions, handle risks, and manage relationships – can accelerate your development as a leader in ways that no other method can. And because the challenges of a job assignment can be especially strong and, at times, even seem overwhelming, it is wise that support from others in the organization accompany them. Some of the more common challenging job assignments are described in the box opposite.

Men report having a greater variety of challenging job assignments than women,[19] which suggests that men may be exposed to more significant learning opportunities. As some other research has indicated, women may have fewer international assignments and are less likely than men to be in roles that give them authority over others. They encounter greater difficulty in obtaining important, "plum" assignments and opportunities to relocate for a better position.[20] As we will see in Chapter 5, research studies on the prevalence of male and female stereotypes have shown that women leaders often lack the presumption of competence given to male leaders. This "double standard" may serve as a barrier to women's attempts to obtain challenging job assignments and perpetuates a vicious cycle that prevents women from receiving the preparation necessary for senior management positions.

How can organizations help men and women learn from job experiences? These assignments are sometimes called "stretch" assignments, and for good reason. They are so effective in leadership development in part because they stretch the individual to the limits of their abilities to achieve goals. They are developmental because leaders may lack the full complement of necessary skills and abilities to perform the job easily. Organizations can help men and women learn from job experiences by giving them support throughout the challenging assignment. Most managers need support from a boss or other parts of the organization to help them overcome deficiencies; it can make the difference between success and failure. Support can provide managers with permission to experiment with new behaviors, confidence to continue to learn, and acceptance and approval from others. A study done by the Corporate Leadership Council[21] found that male leaders placed a higher value on job experiences as a form of development, and women valued coaching, mentoring, and development plans. A winning combination to enable women and men to maximize their learning from challenging job assignments may be to provide coaches and mentors as supportive learning partners along the way.

Coaching

What is coaching? Coaching has emerged as the preferred "just in time" learning to help leaders leverage the areas that have the greatest impact on business results. As described in Valerio & Lee, it is a one-on-one development process formally contracted between a coach and a management-level client to help achieve goals related to professional development and/or business performance.[22] Coaching typically helps leaders improve in self-awareness and self-management through the use of learning through on-job actions. Coaching programs most often involve regular coaching sessions with an external coach for a period of six months to a year or more. Organizations often make the investment in the resources required for coaching for talented women and men who are viewed as having a future potential in the organization. Coaching can have a profound influence by assisting men and women in building self-awareness and managing themselves and others. It enables them to make better decisions for themselves and their organizations in the face of uncertainty, and in so doing, facilitate the emergence of human wisdom. When utilized at the top of large organizations, coaching activities can potentially affect the lives of many, and improve the chances that executives and their teams will be better able to act wisely.[23,24]

How can a coach help? What actually happens in the coaching relationship that allows men and women to get better at interpersonal skills, communicating, delegating, time management, emotional self-management, or other soft skills? How does someone focus on and improve these kinds of skills? With the coach's help, a feedback loop is created based on trying out new behaviors, followed by feedback and reflection, and then trying the new behaviors again to improve effectiveness. Although the names may differ, in almost all one-on-one coaching situations, a coaching process will contain the steps and features shown as a brief outline in the box below.

> ## Good to Know:
> ### Outline of Steps in the Coaching Process[25]
>
> **1. Contracting**
> An understanding is reached with the client about the coaching objectives, measurement of success, reporting and confidentiality, costs.
>
> - Involves discussion and written proposal or letter of agreement.
> - Important roles played by client, boss, HR professional, coach.
>
> **2. Initial Goal Setting**
> Clear goals are set about what is to be accomplished and may be short and/or long term. Coaching objectives may be articulated as leadership competencies needed.
>
> - Expectations are articulated and disagreements are explored.
> - Initial draft of goals may change as coaching process evolves.
>
> **3. Assessment**
> Measures (such as multi-rater feedback, surveys, personality assessments, performance appraisals) are obtained to determine the gap between current performance and future desired performance.
>
> - Client obtains more self-awareness of strengths and development needs.
>
> - Coach and client operate together with common language and set of concepts.
>
> **4. Development Action Planning**
> Client and coach determine how best to leverage strengths and prioritize development needs to impact performance objectives.
>
> - Client's development plan specifies new behaviors to be demonstrated to bosses, direct reports, peers, customers and other stakeholders.
> - With support of coach, client creates time for reflection and tries new behaviors (may use role plays, visioning, problem solving/discussion).
>
> **5. Evaluation**
> Coach and client evaluate what has changed in the areas of client's behavior, what client learned, stakeholder perceptions, client's feelings about the coaching experience.
>
> - Periodic reports enable coach and client to make adjustments in the process.
> - Can determine if allocation of resources yielded results for client and organization.

Although there has been less systematic research on coaching than on other leadership development methods, the available evidence indicates that it is an important tool for helping men and women develop new behaviors that enable them to grow as leaders.[26]

Mentoring

What is mentoring? Mentoring relationships are vital resources for men and women in organizations.[27] They serve as an important source of information exchange and help foster a sense of belonging to the organization. The relationship between the less experienced individual (the protégé) and the more experienced person (the mentor) may benefit both the individuals involved as well as the organization. The mentor may be a supervisor, peer, someone else outside the protégé's management chain, or even an individual in an outside organization. Very often, mentoring relationships occur when the mentor is associated with a dominant, powerful group in the organization and the protégé is associated with a non-dominant, less powerful group. Mentor actions such as support, sponsorship, and visibility to upper management can help protégés learn how to navigate in the organization and often lead to the career advancement of protégés. Having multiple mentors may enhance mentoring outcomes. For many people, mentoring relationships may make the difference between surviving and thriving in any given organization.[28]

Benefits of mentoring for women and men. There has been much research showing that workplace mentoring fosters the professional and personal growth of employees. As explained by Dr. Belle Rose Ragins, Strategic Management Professor at the University of Wisconsin, "Protégés receive greater compensation, more promotions, and more career mobility than those who do not have mentors."[29] The outcomes of mentoring for protégés also may include career commitment, job satisfaction, and self-esteem at work.[30,31,32] Mentoring also provides protégés with a greater sense of competence, identity as a professional, acceptance and confirmation by others. It is not surprising, given the current status of pay inequity in general, that the research has found that gender plays a role in the outcomes for protégés: male mentors are associated with greater protégé compensation than female mentors.[33] Same-gender and cross-gender mentoring relationships may provide the opportunity to learn different things. Both female mentors and protégés report that the focus of same-gender relationships is on the valuable role-modeling that such a situation provides. Women protégés want to find out how other women have dealt with the challenges associated with being a woman *and* a leader. They wish to learn from other women how to move through the labyrinth and be resilient in the face of obstacles. In addition, mentoring relationships can provide a safe haven for exploring how to mesh one's identity as a woman with the requirements of the workplace. When the mentor is not the protégé's supervisor, the mentoring relationship may better enable the protégé to bring her authentic identity to the relationship and allow her to arrive at improved strategies and insights.

With the increase of women in future leadership roles, as more women become mentors for male protégés, there will be greater opportunity for men to gain a better understanding of the perspectives of women leaders. The advantage for men is that it affords them more opportunity for understanding the issues that many women in organizations are facing, and for observing leadership behaviors such as the Big Five Personality Traits and Leadership Styles in women leaders. Both mentors and protégés in diversified mentoring relationships may have a safe place to explore their own assumptions, attitudes, and stereotypes resulting in greater understanding and insights about others.

In mentoring relationships the learning is not one-way. Are there benefits for mentors? You bet! Mentoring can benefit mentors by providing them with knowledge and input from different parts of the organization, a loyal base of support, and a sense of personal satisfaction in nurturing and developing talented individuals. As an added bonus, they get the chance to pass along some hard-earned wisdom and "war stories." No wonder many mentors say they get as much out of the relationship as the protégés!

Informal and formal mentoring. Informal mentoring relationships occur naturally and develop spontaneously, based on mutual liking, interests, and comfort between the mentor and protégé. As you might expect, these informal relationships often produce more of the positive results associated with mentoring relationships. In contrast, formal mentoring relationships are usually the result of a matching process within a company-sponsored mentoring program. Formal mentoring programs can vary in how they are structured, their duration, and funding and support levels by management. Formal workplace mentoring appears to be less effective in promoting personal and career growth than these more spontaneous, informal relationships. Although much has been written about the value to organizations, there is increasing recognition that, whether formal or informal, mentoring relationships offer much personal value for protégés and mentors. The emotional support these relationships provide to both mentors and protégés can help them withstand the stress and uncertainty that accompanies the frequent job transitions in today's workplace.

Leadership Development Programs

What are some characteristics of leadership development programs? Some organizations use formal Leadership Development Programs to help executives and leaders develop their leadership skills in alignment with the organization's business objectives. The concepts, content, and program objectives are designed and developed to address the challenges faced by the target population in attaining the goal of the business. For example, a program for senior executives may be focused on enhancing strategic leadership in a global environment or a program for mid-level managers may help them learn behaviors such as collaboration and teamwork that are more appropriate in less hierarchical organizations. Executives may attend off-site programs that were custom-designed for the organization by internal staff or academic faculty or "open-enrollment" programs that are offered by business schools or leadership institutes that feature a standardized curriculum. Program duration may typically be three to five days and the topics and illustrative business cases are designed to meet the organization's identified strategic needs. Programs typically may use a blend of methods including direct teaching of material by faculty and/or peers and staff, facilitated discussions, experiential learning (using role-plays and case scenarios), multi-rater feedback, and coaching. Interactions with others are balanced with time for reflection. Multi-rater feedback (also called 360-degree feedback) comes from multiple sources such as boss, direct reports, peers, self, clients/customers and is very helpful in providing participants with the perceptions of each of the rater groups.[34]

What are feedback-intensive programs? Behavioral change has a greater likelihood of occurring in feedback-intensive programs in which there is a comprehensive assessment of an individual's leadership.[35] Coaching may be incorporated into the program design during on-site sessions and in later follow-up. Participants may receive their feedback on-site from coaches who assist them with integrating all of the data from various feedback sources and writing a development action plan. Participants can continue the learning process by implementing their action plans on the job over a period of months, facilitated through the follow-up sessions with coaches conducted either in person or by telephone.

For some organizations, as people ascend the hierarchy, the less feedback they receive. That makes these types of programs all the more valuable. Feedback-intensive programs provide rich and comprehensive feedback from a variety of sources such as multi-rater feedback tools, self-assessments from personality and preference questionnaires, leadership style inventories, peer observations from other program participants, participant interviews, and many other leadership assessment instruments. Because women may need more opportunities to obtain feedback about how they are perceived, sending them to feedback-intensive programs may be an especially effective form of leadership development for them.

What are single-identity programs? Among the program options available for women managers are traditional heterogeneous programs or programs tailored specifically for them, known as single-identity programs. Single-identity programs offer additional content dealing with identity issues and complexities arising from career barriers in the labyrinth.[36] Single-identity programs offer many benefits to participants. Women report that they offer a safe, supportive way to share experiences and they can open up about issues that cannot be discussed in mixed company. Many women, particularly those who feel isolated as the solo executive female or who are in male-dominated industries, have few or no other women managers from whom to learn or with whom to socialize. For many, it is a relief to be surrounded by other women who are facing the same challenges. For once, they are in the majority! They may also feel encouraged to try out new behaviors and make mistakes without the intense scrutiny and fear of reprisals that they experience in their jobs. In addition, they may also be able to share concerns with others who have had similar experiences – and learn new coping strategies.[37] Comparison of feedback from back home (which can be predominantly male) with feedback from classroom peers (all-female) helps women understand when stereotypes may be influencing their feed-back and when they may be using prejudice as a convenient excuse to deny their poor performance.

Both women-only and mixed-gender programs enable women to grow as leaders. Making the determination about which type of program to attend may depend on the circumstances that a leader is facing at that particular time in her career.

Summary

This chapter has highlighted recent research on leadership behaviors such as competencies, personality traits, and leadership styles found to be important to men and women in leadership roles. It has enabled you to see that leadership is not a matter of exhibiting stereotypically masculine or feminine traits. There is ample evidence to show that successful leadership requires that both men and women show a combination of characteristics that include intelligence, sociability, assertiveness, conscientiousness, integrity, and the ability to inspire others with their optimistic visions of the future. Although neither men nor women have a lock on leadership, women are more likely to be transformational leaders. Both men and women must work hard to understand their strengths and "challenge areas" to achieve greater self-awareness and self-management – hallmarks of good leaders everywhere.

You have also seen that some of the proven methods that men and women in organizations use to help them develop their leadership are job assignments, coaching, mentoring, and development pro-grams. But men and women need not act alone; they can be assisted in these endeavors by their organizations. The next chapter provides recommendations on what CEOs and Human Resource executives can do to develop talented women.

Part II

Practical Suggestions for Organizations, Managers, and Women

Chapter 4

CEOs and Human Resource Executives Can Develop Talented Women

Chief Executive Officers (CEOs), Human Resource (HR) executives, and their organizations have a major part to play in the drama that is unfolding before our eyes: "Globalization." It is a powerful role on the national and world stage and requires that you take action to diversify your workforce. With the publication of the Hudson Institute's report about the changing demographics of the American labor force entitled "Workforce 2000: Work and Workers for the Twenty-first Century," suddenly diversity initiatives catapulted to the top of the list for many CEOs.[1] Since then, thousands of diversity initiatives have been launched across organizations in all industrial and economic sectors for the new entrants to the workforce: women, people of color, and new immigrants. Diversity has now come to include differences in various social identities such as race, ethnicity, sexual orientation, class, nationality, religion, and even educational background, values, styles, and preferences.

Due in part to globalization, CEOs, HR executives, and their organizations now occupy a unique role in creating policies and practices that have the ability to influence many segments of society. Like water droplets falling into a pool of water, as Figure 4.1 illustrates, the actions taken by CEOs and their organizations have ripple effects that can radiate out from the corporate policies affecting their own employees to policies and practices on both the national and global scene.

Figure 4.1 What CEOs and HR executives can do to develop talented women

And so this chapter is addressed to you, CEOs and HR executives, as you grapple with the decisions that forge change for you and the people in your organizations. In this chapter we will take a look at what you can do to develop talented women and provide you with some examples from best-practice companies. Interspersed are the thoughts and comments from executives interviewed by the author. Because the role you play is so critical to shaping and influencing corporate culture, this chapter offers ideas for you to consider as you make your organization more hospitable for women and others.

Diversity and Inclusion and the Creation of Wealth

Diversity and inclusion are business imperatives. In the past century in the United States, we have moved from a system of legal separation between blacks and whites to the dissolution of legal racism. The women's movement was also partially responsible for many legal and social reforms which have been transforming the nature of gender roles in society. The workforce in organizations has been on the forefront of these changes, challenging the traditional ways of thinking, working, and managing. Some organizations have chosen to be on the leading edge of the societal changes and have functioned as social change agents.[2]

Although not all organizations may wish to function as change agents for society, all organizations must develop their talented women to survive in today's world. Why? One of the most compelling reasons for developing talented women is coming from the change in demographics. As previously mentioned, in the United States women earn the majority of college and Master's degrees and nearly 50% of doctorates. Women are now already a large proportion of the talent available for leadership.

It is that simple. As mentioned in Chapter 2, in the 2004 *Catalyst* "Bottom Line" study[3] there is a positive correlation between the numbers of women in top leadership positions and certain business performance measures. Although correlation does not always imply causation, logic tells us that diversity in leadership makes sense. The driving forces for organizational change, also discussed in Chapter 2, have been flattening and shrinking the globe and bringing together the diverse people of the world. Why shouldn't organizations mirror this diversity by including the variety of perspectives?

Organizations can incorporate new perspectives by acknowledging the importance of gender. One of the tasks facing CEOs and their leadership teams is the development and integration of women into top leadership positions. What your stakeholders need to see from you is an increase in experimentation and flexibility in the way women are perceived and allowed to act. "By becoming more educated, and able to do more productive, higher-wage jobs – women have increased the size of the economic pie ... If you look across countries, education is the strongest predictor for how quickly the pie grows," says Lawrence Katz, a labor economist at Harvard.[4] Organizations that create cultures of equal opportunity for all are better able to attract, retain, and motivate the best available workers on the planet. In so doing, organizations position themselves for what many consider to be their number one purpose: the creation of wealth.

What CEOs and HR Executives Can Do

There are a range of actions that you can take to provide better developmental opportunities for women. Organizations have many tools at their disposal in the form of programs, policies, and procedures that can support women's leadership. Many of the actions discussed in this chapter involve the examination of policies and procedures. Others are related to providing a feedback-rich environment for women, who often do not receive timely, realistic feedback about their work performance. The end result is to make women feel wanted and welcome in the organization. The experiences of women are different from those of their male colleagues, who are more likely to receive informal feedback from their male bosses and peers. In addition, the implementation of practices such as mentoring, multi-rater feedback, executive coaching, and personal feedback from bosses can help women gain a picture of their strengths and challenge areas. As one interviewee noted: "Anything that can help women open their

---

What CEOs and HR Executives Can Do to Develop Talented Women

Fairness Issues

- Communicate the commitment to diversity
- Dedicate budget and resources to diversity
- Make diversity a required consideration in promotion decisions
- Measure performance on gender-related issues
- Hold decision-makers accountable for distributing plum assignments
- Ensure fair performance evaluations

Leadership Development

- Sponsor women's networks
- Provide formal and informal opportunities for mentoring
- Provide external coaches for high-potential women
- Provide external stretch assignments
- Create innovative development programs that provide international experience

Career Design

- Allow greater work flexibility
- Redesign how careers are built

eyes about how they are perceived is important for companies to implement." As with all progressive actions, innovative ideas take time to permeate an organization and become commonly adopted as "the way we do business around here."

The box provides you with a host of actions you can implement that may be clustered into three areas: *Fairness issues, Leadership development*, and *Career design.*

Fairness Issues

Communicate the commitment to diversity by the leadership team. The commitment to diversity starts with the CEO and the Board of Directors. CEOs have a pivotal role to play in creating an organizational climate that fosters productivity, the attraction and development of talented people, and inclusiveness. The commitment to diversity needs to be obvious throughout the organization, starting with the top leadership team and cascading outward. According to one advertising agency CEO, "It is clear that if organizations don't pay attention to this issue they will lose talented women." There are a number of different ways in which a CEO and the top leadership team can demonstrate their commitment.

Place women on boards. CEOs can recommend women candidates to their boards of directors. There appears to be a growing worldwide trend to appoint more women to boards of directors. For example, Norway is meeting a goal set in a 2003 law for 40% of board seats to be held by women by the year 2008. "For women eager to gain a seat in the boardroom, the good news from Norway and elsewhere in Europe is that ... companies are searching for women with qualifications, talent and tact to serve ... There is a new paradigm for corporate governance ..."[5] It makes good sense to place women on boards: they represent 51% of the marketplace and they pay attention to ethics issues. In light of the research that suggests that women may have a stronger moral orientation, placing women on boards may be the organizational equivalent of sending canaries into a coal mine. Women may be more sensitively attuned to ethical violations and more likely to voice their concerns to others when potentially risky business practices threaten the stability of the corporation.

Generate diverse candidate slates. Starting with their direct report team and moving through the organization, CEOs can also demand that selection teams generate gender-diverse candidate slates. Because talent is increasingly in short supply, CEOs can insist that the quest for well-qualified candidates be made a priority throughout all levels of management. Encouraging managers to develop talented people at all levels in the organization helps to insure that there is a steady stream of talent in the pipeline. The CEO together with the top executive team can communicate the importance of diversity and women's leadership to local leaders, and hold individuals (including each other) accountable for progress in this area. In the words of one CEO, "It is important to have women in the pipeline in middle management jobs."

Use metrics. The CEO can call upon the employee opinion survey team to measure the inclusiveness of the organizational climate and to assess the degree to which the organization may be "inhospitable" to women. According to one general manager in a global technology company: "Organizations must build in mechanisms to understand where the barriers are and ... what's getting in the way. Metrics can be used to measure the pipeline, recruitment, retention, and advancement. Surveys and other tools can help make the changes visible over time." There are abundant opportunities for measurement of results here. What is required is a willingness to drill down into the data at lower levels in the organization, and your survey professionals are trained to help out here. Data can be analyzed at the local level to include measures from particular functional units and individual managers. The CEO and top team can set diversity goals and hold managers accountable for increasing the numbers of women in certain positions and/or lowering the turnover rate among women in certain functions.

Dedicate budget and resources to diversity. Increasing women's access to leadership positions requires that an organization devote resources to diversity efforts. These resources include an overall plan for diversity, programs for diversity initiatives, dedicated staff to create and administer the entire initiative, and an adequate budget to support it all. You already know this, but sometimes the hardest part is implementing it successfully because it requires a sustained commitment.

The research tells us that organizations that assign responsibility for diversity see more positive effects from diversity training, and evaluations, networking, and mentoring.[6]

Men as champions of women's development. How can organizations increase the likelihood of their success on diversity matters and increase the cadres of women leaders? By assigning respected, upper-level personnel to lead Diversity departments that report to top leadership. Diversity leaders must have the authority to hold all managers accountable for the success of programs and results in such functions as recruitment, retention, and promotion. Appointing a respected white male as diversity leader may be one way to help increase the involvement of males in the development of women.

Organizations can also take actions that encourage males to be advocates for women. Some organizations, such as Deloitte, communicate the notion of men as "champions" of women's development as a priority for the organization.[7] In their respective roles as the bosses and peers of talented women, many men appreciate an organizational authorization that permits them to be more supportive and advocating for the talented women in their groups. In my work as an executive coach I frequently encounter men who would like to be more helpful in advancing the careers of talented women, but, for many reasons, feel some hesitation in doing so. Group initiatives can enable men to feel more comfortable in learning how to take a greater role in women's career development in their organizations.

Make diversity a required consideration in promotion decisions. As the *Catalyst* research shows, diversity improves the bottom line. During talent reviews, the responsibility and accountability for diversity need to be held by all decision-makers on the team – not just the female members. All managers, both male and female, need to be held accountable for diversity in promotion decisions and can offer names of women for consideration. One female interviewee in the marketing department of a high-tech company said that during the talent reviews conducted for succession planning attended by her manager and peers in her department, "I'm expected to be the one looking out for the advancement of women candidates. My male counterparts in the room rely on me and another female manager to raise the issue of promoting the women in the department. They will not speak up about it, even though we are supposed to have diverse candidate slates. There may be reluctance by male bosses to be as honest as they are about the men because of concerns about sexual harassment complaints."

Having a clear mandate from the top of the organization in addition to fair performance appraisals can enable males to overcome the reluctance to put forward the names of specific talented women. It can also empower men to expand their networks of talented women to become familiar with larger populations of talent in their organizations. As one female general manager for a high-tech company put it: "The men put on the succession lists only the women they know. Male leaders need to spend time in so-called 'non-traditional' environments to see the full range of talent we have. On technical teams especially, it is important for men to get to know many women candidates."

Measure performance on gender-related issues. As many organizations have learned, "You *are* what you *measure!*" Technology now easily enables the measurement of information related to many aspects of equal opportunity. What can be measured? Practically *anything* can be measured: trends in the attitudes and engagement of women, the extent to which an organizational climate is "women-friendly," as well as program objectives in recruitment, hiring, promotion, and retention. Surveys can be designed to measure results at all levels in an organization, even down to the performance record of individual managers for the promotion and advancement of women in their organizations. Surveys are a useful tool to provide detailed analyses of outcomes and trends in the organizational climate. CEOs and their organizations can use them to track the effects of Diversity and Inclusion initiatives, help them determine annual strategic objectives, and allocate resources for leadership development initiatives.

As is the case for all survey efforts, however, CEOs and their leadership teams must be prepared to address the issues that will arise as a result of merely *asking* the questions. As one of the interviewees, a general manager, said: "Organizations must understand the diversity of thought on various issues. They need to know what their constituency mix should be and to understand what is getting in the way through the use of surveys. Then they have to make visible the 'change-making.'"

One company that has a rich history in the area of Diversity and Inclusion is PepsiCo. With oversight by the CEO and top executives, the Diversity councils and subcommittees have created multiple approaches to address women's needs and measure the results of initiatives. PepsiCo's Organizational Health Surveys measure progress through the use of questions in the areas of work–life harmony, career, and inclusion. Examples of some survey questions are given in the box below.

Best Practices
Questions from *PepsiCo's* Organizational Health Survey[8,9]

- "My company supports my efforts to balance my work and personal life."
- "I feel this is a company where I can have a successful career."
- "Since PepsiCo implemented Inclusion training, I have seen improvements in our culture, it is more inclusive."
- "Senior management (your senior leadership team) has taken ownership for the company's diversity and inclusion initiatives."
- "My manager supports and encourages my involvement in diversity and/or inclusion related activities."
- "I see diversity reflected in the management of this company."
- "My manager recognizes diversity as a business imperative and takes specific actions to drive it."
- "My work group has a climate in which diverse perspectives are valued."

Measurement against norms. There is an opportunity here for survey consortium groups and vendors responsible for survey design and the maintenance of industry and company norms to elevate knowledge levels about best practices in Diversity and Inclusion. Survey norms can be created against which companies can measure themselves and compare themselves to "best practice" organizations. For example, the existence of hotlines to encourage whistle-blowing to report unethical, discriminatory, or other inappropriate behavior has dramatically increased over the last decade. The Mayflower Group (a consortium of Fortune 100 companies that share survey norms and best practices in HR) collected data indicating what percentage of member companies reported having a hotline.[10]

Include diversity objectives on performance appraisals. Most performance appraisals include a combination of business and "people" objectives. Some organizations include diversity and inclusion objectives in their performance management processes and hold managers accountable for achieving these objectives. PepsiCo introduced two discrete appraisal ratings – People Objectives and Business Objectives – to measure managers' performance. The dual rating practice provides strong accountability for managers to perform in both areas. Senior executives are required to have at least one or more inclusion-related People Objectives.[11]

For any performance management system to be effective, managers must be held accountable for their behavior. If individual managers consistently fail to achieve diversity objectives, their managers may recommend that they attend more diversity training or receive some coaching. In some cases, organizations may consider the use of other appropriate options to assist employees in meeting objectives. In summary, using existing technologies, there are many opportunities for organizations to measure the results of initiatives to increase the pools of talented women.

Hold decision-makers accountable for distributing plum assignments. In most organizations for both general manager and functional expert career tracks, there are key jobs and experiences that are critical to future success in leadership roles. Often these are line jobs with profit and loss responsibility, and they may even be "must haves" for candidates being considered for leadership positions. A survey involving CEOs of Fortune 500 companies found that lack of line management experience was cited as the top barrier to advancement for women.[12] How might you insure that key assignments get distributed to the talented women in your organization? What is the organizational influence on and oversight into the distribution of these plum assignments?

Some questions you may want to ask are:

- Which assignments carry greater visibility to senior management, committees, and boards?
- What mechanisms are in place to adequately prepare women to be comfortable in front of these committees and boards, especially when, at this point in time, they are frequently the only female in the room?

- Because women are often required to avoid directive and assertive behavior and to avoid self-promotion,[13] how might you and your organization insure that women are considered for these important developmental experiences?
- What is the organizational infrastructure in place to support women's success, such as development programs, mentoring, and coaching?

Ensure fair performance evaluations. Left to their own devices, people prefer to associate with those who resemble them in physical and personal characteristics, social background, and attitudes. It makes sense then to adopt methods that limit subjectivity and bias in performance evaluations. It's just good practice to hold managers accountable for evaluating performance on the basis of valid evidence of results and accomplishments. Without a mandate for clear standards applied uniformly to all candidates, people making decisions about hiring and promotion often unwittingly operate solely in their comfort zone and rely on the familiar.

How can organizations reduce bias in judgments and safeguard against stereotypic bias? To ensure fairer evaluations, organizations can impose corporate oversight and accountability. The performance appraisal can be constructed to include sections that describe not only the business results achieved but also ratings of behaviors (in the form of descriptive, behaviorally anchored rating scales) based on clear definitions of leadership competencies.

Of course, training on how to rate and administer the performance appraisal is critical to successful implementation. Training on the implementation of performance evaluations can also include helping managers understand how stereotypes can influence judgments about people. This is especially important when making judgments about women because of the tendency to equate leadership with men and not women.[14]

Raising awareness of biases to a conscious level may mean that organizations require managers to take a second look at the performance evaluations of women when they evaluate them and to scrutinize the evaluations of men and women when there are discrepancies in pay in the same job.[15]

Training in performance evaluations should also include helping managers overcome their reluctance to deliver candid feedback.

Managers can learn to give both positive and constructive feedback that enables employees to receive a realistic view of their performance.

Leadership Development

Sponsor women's networks. Women value the opportunity to share their experiences with other women. One organizational strategy involves sponsoring women's networks that host a variety of activities such as seminars, speaker series, workshops, and informal opportunities for women to socialize with each other. These can take the form of local round tables, "brown-bag lunch" sessions with featured speakers, blogs, and webcasts. Women's networks offer obvious advantages to both the participants and the organization. Participants may learn more about specific skills, career advancement strategies, organizational politics, and what it takes to be successful in the company. In the words of one interviewee from a large consumer products company, "Earlier in my career I wasn't clued into the subtleties of office politics that men know. Organizations can benefit from programs that enable women to build their relationships and networks across departments."

Because there have been fewer female role models at high levels in organizations, women need to learn more about how other women were successful and managed to achieve their professional goals. Getting to know other women also serves to reduce a sense of isolation felt by many women. These networks usually encourage mentoring and offer opportunities for mentoring relationships to evolve that are based on natural affinities between people and "chemistry." Often held during regular business hours, rather than the evening hours, when family responsibilities prohibit many women from lingering later into the evening, these networking groups also benefit the organization. In the words of one interviewee, "The networking groups consist of both junior and senior women so they can learn from each other." Enabling women to get to know each other better across divisions or global functional teams increases the communication channels needed to get work done. Said another, "We do a women's program to create the network and give participants a view of themselves as leaders. The network is global and goes across functions and levels."

Use of technology and social networking. Companies are now using technology to forge connectivity among women globally. For example, to help build the pipeline of women leaders worldwide in IBM, in 2006 the "Super Women's Group" was created. The technology includes tools for the virtual community such as interactive presentations, social networking, and an online information repository designed to educate high-potential women on leadership and career development opportunities. It enables women and men to learn from those who have been successful within the company. The group has hosted interactive blogs with women leaders to share experiences, tips, and advice to help each other with the challenges they face. Virtual networking calls (podcasts) and local chapters have been established in such locations as China, India, and Thailand.

Some of the topics discussed on the tens of thousands of registrations for the virtual calls are included in the box below. Although springboarded through a women's initiative, it is important to note that this conduit is definitely not just "For Women Only" – the topics are so relevant to the entire workforce that many numbers of men call in as well!

Best Practices
**Topics Discussed on *IBM's Super Women's Group*
Webcast Event Series**[16]

- Personal branding and you
- Having a successful career while working remotely
- Establishing a network as an experienced hire
- How to squeeze in a workout while working 60-hour weeks
- "I'm so much cooler online": Managing in today's virtual environment
- Becoming a dynamic speaker
- Getting the most out of your mentoring relationships
- 10 Things I wish I knew earlier!
- Balancing career and family
- Building up your confidence
- Making time for community service
- Getting the most out of your mentoring relationships

Another company that utilizes multiple approaches to address women's needs is PepsiCo. Special focus is on two areas: Connectivity and Work–Life Harmony. Among the initiatives for Connectivity is the PepsiCo Women's Connection Website. The website provides input from women's groups across PepsiCo globally and has links to local network sites. Some of the areas determined to be of interest to the target audience within PepsiCo are given in the box below.

Best Practices
PepsiCo's Women's Connection Website Highlights
What are Women Looking for?[17]

- Career advice from senior PepsiCo women
- Articles on topics such as careers, networking, balance, etc.
- Discussion forums to share best practices for managing career, building relationships with PepsiCo women, personal networking (e.g., connect with other working mothers, find an exercise partner, etc.)
- Opportunity to submit questions and receive responses from the CEO and other senior women
- Bibliography of resources for women
- Professional biographies of senior women from PepsiCo
- Profiles of successful women outside PepsiCo

Provide formal and informal opportunities for mentoring. Organizations can set up formal mentoring programs in which mentors are matched with protégés on a variety of different criteria. Some mentoring programs bring people together through social events, so they can meet and pair naturally. Others set up structured programs that designate periods of time when mentor and protégé can meet together. Good formal programs have procedures for changing partners and for either party to end the relationship without retribution.[18] Some programs rely on supervisors to match mentor and protégé, but this may be somewhat limited to the supervisor's own network of colleagues and friends in the organization.

Companies can also use leadership development programs to enhance the informal opportunities for mentoring. In one of the leadership development programs offered in the pharmaceutical company, Bristol-Myers Squibb, participants learn how to gain greater organizational savvy. Assisting in this effort are the "alumni" of the program who are invited to join in an evening discussion session to further expand the networking and mentoring opportunities.[19]

Whether the opportunity for mentoring is offered formally or informally, what is important here is that mentoring can serve as an important socialization and acculturation function and a vehicle for an exchange of information: women learn more about how to be successful in the organization, and the organization, in turn, learns more about its employees' talent, needs, and capabilities.

Create innovative development programs that provide international experience. At one time, you could "get your ticket punched," literally and figuratively, by doing a stint in a company's overseas office. But more recently, as an alternative to spending one to three years in an international assignment to obtain the job experience of working internationally and understanding different cultures, some organizations are experimenting with less time-consuming and costly alternatives. Rather than spend time selecting candidates for international assignments, paying costs associated with relocation, acculturation training, and repatriation, assignments may be structured for three- to six-month periods of time with assignees returning home for frequent visits. However, in the words of one director in a large aerospace company who manages over 1,000 people globally: "Organizations must understand the needs of women and provide good infrastructure. If people cannot do a special rotational assignment, the organization must find out what other options are out there."

Some organizations are trying out other alternatives. In one such innovative program, high-potential people at IBM can develop their leadership by working on teams that will be deployed to four-week projects in various countries around the globe. IBM's program, which it calls the Corporate Service Corps, "Gives IBM a high profile in countries where it does not yet have a significant presence." After their four-week trips, "the participants will go through … intensive debriefing to discuss what they learned about leadership – and about the countries they visited. 'It feels good to help in a developing country, even as you enhance your career,' said Julie T. Lockwood, a manager in Boulder, CO. 'This will help my internal resume more than an assignment in a developed country.'"[20]

Provide external stretch assignments. Sometimes managers learn valuable lessons about leadership from roles they assume outside the workplace. External stretch assignments enable leaders to gain experiences not available within the organization. Loaned executives may work with volunteers to manage employee campaigns in businesses, government, and professional firms. An example has been the United Way's Loaned Executive program in which executives on loan work as members of the United Way for a given period of time.

Other stretch experiences include roles requiring public speaking and serving on boards. Speaking at professional and industry meetings and serving on non-profit boards can build confidence and provide deeper insights into organizational politics. Such assignments can offer women the opportunity to increase the scope of their networks outside the organization. "Serving on a board gives you insight into how things work at high levels," one interviewee said. Some interviewees also reported that giving presentations to external groups helped them develop "executive presence" and greater confidence when speaking in front of large groups. Others reported that it expanded both their knowledge base and their ability to influence others, although juggling multiple roles and jobs remained very challenging.

Provide external coaches for high-potential women. Coaching has become well established as a management practice in all types of organizations throughout the world. Many coaching assignments are initiated to help talented people make significant contributions and grow as executives, rather than "fix" problems. Most of my work as an executive coach involves coaching men and women whom their organizations view as "high-potential." Coaching is useful particularly when someone is facing a business challenge and needs to learn to do things in new ways. This challenge may appear as an increase in the scope of work, a promotion, or any assignment with a high degree of complexity and ambiguity to it. Coaching tends to be most appropriate to help people develop in the "soft" skills areas as shown in the box below.

Good to Know:
When is Coaching Appropriate?[21]

Coaching is appropriate when a person needs help with:

- Building relationships, creating trust, working with peers, working in teams
- Developing direct reports, providing vision and strategy, delegating
- Setting and enforcing standards, handling conflict, calling tough decisions

- Providing recognition and reward, giving feedback, coaching others
- Improving time management and work–life integration

Coaching accelerates the learning process and can be helpful for women as they make their way through the labyrinth by providing them with more feedback about their performance and how they are perceived by others in the organization. For example, women can develop strategies so that they may be viewed as more decisive and direct. It can also help the organization demonstrate a commitment to diversity and foster the retention of talented women. In the words of one female senior vice president of a technology company: "Coaches have helped me in the past and I wouldn't be where I am today without them." Her sentiments were echoed by many of the interviewees.

Career Design

Allow greater work flexibility. Technology now erases the time barriers around the globe and allows speeds of human communication never before experienced by previous generations. Various technologies now permit work to be done 24/7. While this has had both advantages and disadvantages for individuals in the workforce, it also permits us to restructure and reevaluate how we work. The measurement of tangible results and the overall value of an employee's contributions now trumps "face time" at work as a criterion for performance.

Job restructuring. Job restructuring can include working from home (telecommuting), job sharing, and part-time work. Organizations can examine job tasks and redesign jobs to create more efficiency and to improve the fit with employees' knowledge, skills, and abilities and the required job tasks. Redesigned jobs can also tap into new markets of qualified job candidates, thus benefiting employer and employee alike.

Work reentry programs. Organizations can also consider programs that enable easier reentry after a hiatus from work. Women and men who have taken extended time off for child-rearing or eldercare can be offered training, internships, and part-time work experiences prior to their return to full-time work. Similar to a "new-hire orientation," organizations can offer training to update returning managers on recent changes in the company and industry. Programs that allow people to ease back into full-time schedules can refresh previously learned skills and give families time to make adjustments as they integrate work and life activities. When the American Bar Association (ABA) recognized this issue, members organized a pilot project, "Back to business law," to provide seminars and informal networking opportunities for business lawyers who had left active practice but were still interested in corporate law. The group has a website at backtobusinesslaw.org. The ABA project is similar to others begun by several business schools.[22] In the words of one of the interviewees: "Family care is one of the biggest hurdles for companies to deal with. Women are still the primary caretakers of children and elders, and if companies don't figure out ways to take care of them, companies will lose women."

Flexible work arrangements. Since the 1980s, many companies have had Flexible Work Arrangement (FWA) policies in place. Some examples of FWAs, also termed "family-friendly policies," are flextime, telecommuting, reduced hours/part-time work, compressed work week, and job sharing. Helping employees meet the demands of increasingly complex lives, these arrangements have constituted an improvement over the prior custom of an inflexible, rigidly defined work schedule. Organizational goals of family-friendly programs include attracting new employees, improving retention, increasing productivity, and decreasing stress.

Although these arrangements may be very beneficial for some individual employees and employers, the research findings on the overall success of these programs have been mixed and hampered by methodological problems. The measurements of success have focused on addressing business/organizational needs (e.g., lower absenteeism, increased productivity) rather than the needs of employees (e.g., career satisfaction, work–life integration) or some combination of both. Further studies are necessary to investigate how FWAs are meeting both employee and business needs.[23]

From a practical standpoint, FWAs have a number of limitations.[24] One of the most serious limitations of FWAs is that men view them as being for women only. Making FWAs work at more senior levels is extremely difficult and many companies will not consider employees on reduced-hour FWAs for advancement to upper-level positions. They are neither integrated into nor supported by most talent management processes and those who take FWAs face subtle bias regarding their competence and career commitment. Managers report that FWAs complicate their evaluations of the work performance of employees. Because they are frequently short-term, one-off solutions, FWAs are often viewed as exceptions or accommodations to an outmoded standard. There remains much to be learned about how to make these arrangements work well.

Redesign how careers are built. Integration of work and non-work demands is a critical challenge facing both organizations and employees today. In part due to the fast pace of technology and globalization, there is a structural mismatch between employers' job demands and employees' needs and responsibilities. Too many employees today, both men and women, experience an emotional "tug-of-war" in trying to juggle the demands of work life and personal life. To overcome twentieth-century legacies of outmoded work arrangements, meet the increasing needs of employees for greater work–life integration, and achieve their vision for the future, employers want to remain resilient for the twenty-first century.

For CEOs and their organizations to remain resilient in the face of both technological and social change, they may consider taking a more holistic, systemic strategy by redesigning how careers are built. One such approach is offered by another best practice company, the professional services firm Deloitte.[25,26,27] In the book, *Mass Career*

Customization: Aligning the Workplace with Today's Non-traditional Workforce, authors Cathleen Benko and Anne Weisberg discuss the root causes of the misalignment between today's workplace and the workforce, and show how the corporate ladder model of career progression is already giving way to what Benko and Weisberg call the *corporate lattice™*, a more fluid, adaptive model. They propose a framework called mass career customization (MCC)™[28] that organizations can use to effectively manage that transition.

The MCC framework articulates a definite, not infinite, set of options along four inter-related career dimensions – Pace, Workload, Location/Schedule, and Role – and provides a structure to articulate and manage these options as commonplace events rather than as one-off accommodations. In collaboration with their managers, employees customize their careers by periodically selecting options along each dimension based on their career objectives and current life circumstances within the context of the needs of the business. These mutually agreed-upon choices are registered on a Profile, as illustrated in Figure 4.2.

The profile provides a snapshot of each employee's career at a given point of time and can be adjusted *over* time. Just like you would move the sliders up and down on a stereo equalizer to adjust the sound, MCC allows employees to dial up and down along the four career dimensions to optimize their career paths at varying life stages. In this way, MCC provides a framework for acknowledging that careers ebb and flow, as both people's needs and desires change and the needs and expectations of the business change. The result is a career "sine wave" of sorts, as depicted in Figure 4.3.

Deloitte piloted MCC from 2005 to 2007 and, as of this writing, is well into the roll-out of MCC to all U.S.-based employees.[29] Among key learnings to date:

- MCC has led to more consistent and robust career conversations.
- There is a positive correlation between MCC and employee satisfaction and retention.
- The "dial down" floodgates did not materialize – in fact, MCC has resulted in an increased window into those who want to "dial up" or accelerate their growth.

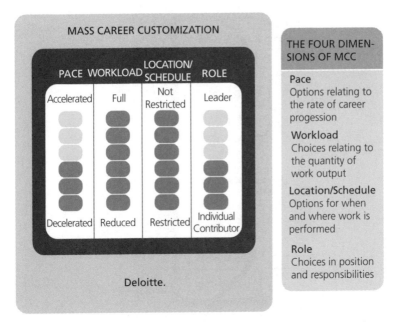

MASS CAREER CUSTOMIZATION

PACE	WORKLOAD	LOCATION/ SCHEDULE	ROLE
Accelerated	Full	Not Restricted	Leader
Decelerated	Reduced	Restricted	Individual Contributor

Deloitte.

THE FOUR DIMENSIONS OF MCC

Pace
Options relating to the rate of career progession

Workload
Choices relating to the quantity of work output

Location/Schedule
Options for when and where work is performed

Role
Choices in position and responsibilities

(Reprinted with permission; from Mass Career Customization: Aligning the Workplace with Today's Nontraditional Workforce, Harvard Business School Publishing, 2007)

Figure 4.2 MCC profile
Source: Benko & Weisberg (2007). Reprinted with permission.

Ultimately, Deloitte has found that one of MCC's greatest benefits is the option value it creates – the comfort of choosing to customize careers as priorities change over time.

Summary

In summary, organizations can create a climate for diversity and inclusion. Organizations can review policies to see if they might be obstacles to the advancement of women. Several of those interviewed felt that companies can be more open-minded so that both women and men can perform their jobs with greater flexibility. We know that

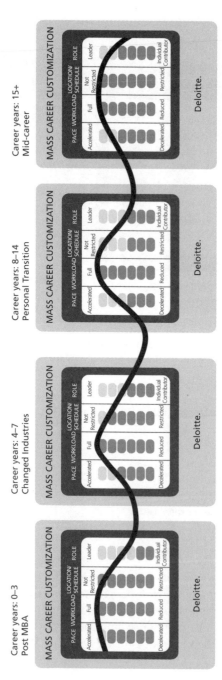

Figure 4.3 MCC wave profile
Source: Benko & Weisberg (2007). Reprinted with permission.

(Reprinted with permission; from Mass Career Customization: Aligning the Workplace with Today's Nontraditional Workforce, Harvard Business School Publishing, 2007)

the type of climate that is created by an organization influences business outcomes and productivity and provides the context for managerial decisions. Once an organization sets the stage for what it can do to develop talented women, then managers can take their cues accordingly. In the next chapter we will find out more about what managers can do to develop talented women.

Chapter 5

What Managers Can Do to Develop Talented Women

Managers can have great impact on the lives of the people who report to them. To get more of an idea about the impact you as a manager can have on the lives of others, take the quiz in the box below. Who were the best bosses you ever had? Many of us can quickly identify our best managers and why we enjoyed working with them.

A Key Developmental Experience:
Who Were Your Best Bosses?

Can individual managers really make a difference? To try this out, jot down the answers to the following three questions:

1. As you think about all of your work or educational experiences, who were the two or three best leaders/managers you ever had?
2. What were the attributes that made them so good?
3. How did they make you feel about yourself?

When asked these questions, most people can recall the outstanding leaders in their lives and are able to list the characteristics that made them so. A couple of the important points for you to note here are that the experience of having a "good boss" cannot be underrated and that, as a manager, you can have a great impact on another person. In what is now classic research done by the Center for Creative Leadership, managers defined it as one of the key developmental experiences in their careers.[1]

Many of us have experienced firsthand how a "good boss" can influence the trajectory of our careers and touch our lives with their wisdom. Even in private coaching conversations, executives speak with reverence about the managers whose guidance helped them along the way. And it is not surprising that one characteristic that is exhibited by many effective leaders is a genuine interest in developing others. Many fine leaders understand the importance of fostering leadership in others and, in so doing, building organizational capability. As a person's manager, the impact that you can have on someone else's career and life has the potential to be very significant, and is a responsibility not to be taken lightly or underestimated.

But unfortunately, many managers, both male and female, could be more comfortable in developing others, particularly when those "others" are women. This chapter is addressed to managers and is designed to help you understand how to be better at developing talented women. It offers some ideas to help you understand how to understand and overcome some of your own hidden biases that prevent you from achieving your business objectives through the work of others in your organization. It also offers you some questions for your own reflection to help you think through your own situation and arrive at some solutions.

In this chapter we will look at "dual-gender" actions that can be taken by both male and female managers, as well as "separate-gender" actions – that focus on what male managers can do as distinct from what female managers can do – to develop talented women. Serving as a foundation for your understanding of these actions is the published research selected and deemed most relevant from a vast literature on the applicable topics.

Topics covered in this chapter include the following:

- Social-Relational Contexts at Work
- Best Practices in Talent Management
- Stereotypical Thinking
- Gender Stereotypes
- Why Is It Critical for Managers to Understand Stereotypes?
- What the Research Tells Us
- What Can Managers Do?

- Dual-Gender Actions
- Actions by Men
- Actions by Women

Social-Relational Contexts at Work

Years ago, when I was doing interviews for another project, several male managers confided to me that when they identified a talented woman whom they wanted to mentor and develop as leaders, other male managers in the organization would insinuate that they had "ulterior motives." In the words of one male manager: " Every so often there comes along a talented woman in my organization whom I have wanted to help get ahead, but each time I have tried, my male colleagues have accused me of having an affair with the woman. So I have refrained from helping because I can't take the chance that my actions could be misconstrued in any way." The jocularity expressed by his male colleagues was a subtle form of discrimination, although it went unrecognized as such at the time. It was also a misfortune on many levels – for the organization that was wasting its talent, for the individuals who could have benefited from his help, and also for him, because he would not have the opportunity for personal gratification that many people experience in mentoring others. Organizations have come to recognize that there is great value in encouraging the *mutual* learning that occurs between mentor and protégé and have set up formal and informal mentoring programs as part of talent management processes.

Best Practices in Talent Management

Companies vary in the degree to which they have allocated resources to talent management, diversity, and inclusion. Some companies are considered "best practice" companies and have developed the infrastructure that nurtures and rewards the development of talented individuals. A brief overview of what "best practice" companies do to encourage talent management is found in the box overleaf. Chapter 3 provides greater detail on some of these practices and on how effective leaders, whether male or female, must demonstrate a range of leadership competencies and styles to suit different management situations.

Best Practices in Talent Management:
How Is Talent Managed in "Best Practice" Companies?

Fortunately, in today's world, managers in most large and mid-size organizations spend a great deal of time thinking about the talent in their organizations: how to attract, recruit, and retain talented individuals. The "war for talent" that erupted at the start of the twenty-first century has resulted in the allocation of significant resources to talent management departments which now encompass recruitment, selection, assessment, training, leadership and executive development, and organizational capability. With the focus on the value of leadership, many organizations have adopted structured programs dedicated to developing their people, such as internal and external executive development programs, mentoring, networking, and coaching. Because these programs are designed for groups, rather than individuals, they can function to institutionalize the process of helping another person's career development. They avoid the appearance of impropriety and make it safer and more acceptable for men and women to mentor those of the opposite gender.

Whether your organization engages in best practices or not, at some point, given your limited time and resources as a manager, you must make a decision about who should receive the available development opportunities. How much time and energy can you invest in the development of people? What are the organizationally sanctioned ways in which you may encourage leadership in women? What degree of risk are you willing to take, based on your belief in a talented woman's ability and motivation to succeed? In this chapter we will look at some of the actions that you, as a manager, can take to develop talented women.

Stereotypical Perceptions

In order to learn about the pivotal role that managers can play in the development of women, it is important first to understand more about how stereotypical perceptions and gender bias can influence decision making and the "double bind" that exists for women as leaders. Why is this important to know? Because the research shows how stereotypical thinking leads to subtle forms of discrimination toward women.

Women's opportunities for advancement to leadership positions have been constrained by gender stereotypes, a lack of performance feedback, and inadequate access to powerful professional networks. This chapter will help you understand the important role you play in influencing both the direction of many women's careers and in building your organization's capability to attract and retain talent. In helping women to overcome these constraints, you yourself can avoid some of the pitfalls frequently encountered by both male and female managers who direct the work of women. These ideas for what managers can do to develop talented women have come from reports about effective practices in leading-edge companies and from the voices of the women and men in my interviews. By the end of this chapter you will agree that it may be time to resurrect one of the fundamental, but often forgotten dictums of good management practice: Get acquainted with the unique set of abilities of each of your direct reports.

Good to Know:
What Are Stereotypes and What Makes Them Dangerous?

Key points:

- Stereotypes are shortcuts used by the brain to group large amounts of data from our complex social world into generalizations about others. Stereotypes are generalizations about individuals' characteristics, the most common of which relate to gender, race/ethnicity, nationality, and occupation. Generalizations can help you make predictions about how others will behave and hence, how you might adjust your own behaviors in our interactions with them.
- One of the dangers of stereotypes is that you are often not aware that you are using stereotypes and the extent to which stereotypes may bias your judgment and decision making.

Stereotypical perceptions can lead to subtle forms of discrimination and in some situations can be a basis for legal claims of discrimination.

- Most of the time, stereotypical thinking operates below your levels of conscious awareness. Stereotypes are resistant to change, so you will be more likely to notice and recall information that confirms prior assumptions than information that contradicts them.
- Stereotypes can cause failures in seeing reality accurately and in understanding the uniqueness of every individual. The overall end result is the very thing you were trying to avoid in the first place: making serious mistakes in your interactions with others owing to a lack of knowledge and incorrect assumptions.

Gender Stereotypes

Some of the most pervasive stereotypes relate to our classification of people according to gender. As we all know, it is a common practice in our culture to assign different colors to newborn babies: pink for girls, blue for boys. So from the very start of life, it is important for us to know the gender of an individual because it tells us how to relate to that tiny person. We use it as a shortcut in creating our expectations about appropriate masculine and feminine behaviors that continue throughout the life span. Even in our modern postindustrial society, there are differences in how parents encourage gender-typed activities and interests, for example in gender-typed toys, games, and household chores.[2] Girls and boys are socialized into the appropriate gender roles through reinforcement/reward for correct behaviors and learning from observations of role models such as parents, the extended family, and others in the social community.

It is no surprise that gender, therefore, is so fundamental to our making sense of the world. From early in our development, we have "schemas" that are both fixed and modifiable patterns through which we perceive the world and respond to it around us.[3] As adult men and women we bring these schemas to organizations and co-create the environments in which we work and live.

Stereotypes about Men and Women

Stereotypes are often built around the characteristics that are required when members of groups perform in typical roles. In their book, *Standing at the Crossroads: Next Steps for High-Achieving Women*, researchers Marian Ruderman and Patricia Ohlott identify five themes (further discussed in Chapter 7) that capture the issues faced by high-achieving women. Two of these themes, *Agency* and *Connection/Communion*, have special relevance for understanding how gender stereotypes may affect men and women.[4]

Connection/Communion refers to our need to be close to others, to remain connected to family, friends, and co-workers. It includes behaviors such as cooperation and taking care of others. People often associate women with the domestic role involving child-rearing and maintaining harmony in the home. Expectations for women are that they will maintain relationships with others and be helpful and nurturing.

Agency refers to acting assertively on one's own behalf, self-sufficiently and independently from others. The contrasting stereotype for men is performance in their employment role as authority figures, leaders, "breadwinners." Expectations for men are that they will be assertive, aggressive, self-reliant, and tough. It includes behaviors such as self-promotion, autonomy, and questioning ideas that do not meet needs.

Connection/Communion has been associated with qualities considered to be feminine, while *Agency* has been associated with masculinity. For a quick summary of these terms, see the box.

Good to Know:
Agentic and *Communal* Behaviors

- *Communal:* connecting with others, cooperative, interpersonally sensitive, empathetic, and nurturing.

- *Agentic:* assertive, autonomous, self-promoting, dominant, and tough.

Why Is It Critical for Managers to Understand Gender Stereotypes?

In the world of work, holding on to gender stereotypes can have serious consequences for both men and women, and particularly for their managers and the organizations in which they work. Accepting gender stereotypes is akin to having blinders on – they limit vision and permit the wearer to see only a narrow portion of the real world. Effective leadership requires that managers see the big picture with a full panoramic perspective! Stereotypes narrow the range of behaviors that are deemed acceptable and allowable, and they disadvantage both men and women. As you will see in the next section, the research shows that stereotypes are particularly disadvantageous for women.

What the Research Tells Us

As Eagly and Carli discuss in their book, *Through the Labyrinth*, different types of gender bias can lead us to underestimate the performance of talented women. The box overleaf lists examples of gender biases to avoid.[5] In the text that follows they are explained further.

Good to Know: Gender Biases to Avoid	
• The Double Bind • The Double Standard	• Women's Competence Questioned • Resistance to Women's Leadership

The Double Bind for Women

As mentioned in Chapter 3, in the "think manager – think male" mindset, leaders are viewed as possessing more *agentic* or masculine attributes than *communal*, or feminine ones. Men view managerial skill as more characteristic of men than of women.[6,7] As "atypical leaders," women find themselves at an impasse, caught in the "double bind," in which contradictory demands are made of them. On the one hand, when women adopt more *agentic* behaviors, they may be seen as too "aggressive" or "strident"; and on the other hand, when women adopt more communal behaviors, they may be seen as too "soft" or "not tough enough." The double bind requires women to avoid assertive and directive behavior and to demonstrate communal behaviors.[8] But when women act in ways that are consistent with the feminine stereotype, they can be seen as too nice! Men who reported helping their organizations beyond the requirements of their jobs received more promotions, unlike women.[9] Men may receive the benefits of being caring and helping because their behavior was viewed as above and beyond what was expected, whereas helping behaviors are simply expected of women. A 2007 *Catalyst* report, aptly titled, "The Double Bind Dilemma for Women in Leadership: Damned if You Do, Doomed if You Don't," discusses different gender biases and several of the "double bind" predicaments faced by women leaders.[10]

The Double Standard

Given the different expectations for males and females, it is no surprise that we see different sets of standards used to judge the behaviors of men and women. Women who lead in an autocratic (directive) manner receive less favorable evaluations than women who lead in a democratic (participative) manner. Studies involving evaluations of leaders have shown that women are rated lower when they adopt more "masculine," directive styles, particularly when the evaluators are men or the leadership role is one typically occupied by men.[11]

In contrast, men receive equally favorable evaluations regardless of their use of an autocratic (directive) or democratic (participative) style.[12] These dominant behaviors include speaking in a loud voice, having a stern expression, direct disagreement, and verbal or non-verbal interruptions, among others. Leadership roles require managers to wield influence and, depending on the management situation, at times be directive, and so every woman must find the right balance of *agentic* and *communal* behaviors that works for her, otherwise she pays a high price.[13] Women who are seen as too aggressive, dominant, self-promoting, and "pushy" are straying too far from the expected feminine behaviors and can be perceived as threatening to others.

Hence, although men are allowed to boast about their accomplishments, women must avoid using self-promotion as a channel in communicating their achievements to others. Instead, women must resort to demonstrating competence in a less direct manner by being more subtle and diplomatic. An additional pressure on women leaders can occur when supervising other women, whose job roles are more "traditional," such as executive assistants who may be more accustomed to working with assertive male bosses. Women leaders often report that they must balance their agentic behaviors with the need to be perceived as "one of the girls" by talking about some of the interests commonly shared by women.

Women's Competence Questioned

Women leaders often lack the presumption of competence given to male leaders. The jokes and anecdotes about women having to work harder and be better than men in similar positions have some truth to them and have actually been borne out in the research.[14] Despite evidence that women perform as effectively as men in leadership roles, women have to consistently prove their qualifications and credibility. Men's competence as leaders is taken for granted – men are viewed as "natural leaders," whereas women often need to prove over and over again that they can lead.[15,16,17,18] In a large study with nearly five hundred upper-level managers, women in line jobs were the most negatively evaluated of all managers in the sample, receiving lower performance ratings than women in staff jobs or men in either line or staff jobs. In addition, for women to get promoted, their performance had to be regarded as more stellar. Women who got promoted had received higher performance ratings than promoted men, suggesting that women were held to higher standards for promotion. "The relationship between performance ratings and promotions was weaker for men than for women."[19]

The results of these studies have special significance for women and their managers. Women may experience more gender-based bias in their attempts to obtain line jobs, necessary proving-grounds for upper management jobs. Then, once women are actually in the line jobs, they may face other hazards, such as the likelihood of more negative performance ratings. The harsh reality is that questioning women's competence can serve as an obstacle in women's attempts to obtain important jobs, influence others, and attain leadership roles in organizations.

These results reinforce the need for women to receive support in challenging job assignments, as we saw in Chapter 3. One of the senior vice presidents interviewed talked about providing support to a talented woman: "I have an ambitious young woman who wants to take on a hard task as a project. When I talk with my peers about it, I will point to her tenacity to accomplish it against all odds. For a woman to get attention, she needs to demonstrate superordinate experience."

Resistance to Women's Leadership

One of the difficult tasks facing women is to try to find the correct mix of *agentic* and *communal* behaviors so that they can decrease the risk of social disapproval by moving outside the narrow band[20] of acceptable behavior. At times this band narrows so much that many women feel that they are walking on a tightrope. One slight misstep and they can tumble downward! Certainly the behavior of women leaders is under greater scrutiny than that of their male counterparts. When women show behaviors that are outside the prescriptive gender norms, they may be disliked and encounter resistance to their leadership by others.[21] This resistance to their leadership is particularly difficult for women because in order to be leader-like and influential, a woman must be likeable.

How do women increase their chances for "likeability" and reduce their chances for resistance to their leadership? Yep, you guessed it – display greater warmth and collaboration. Women who display communal behaviors such as smiling, expressing agreement, warmth, and showing support of others and a willingness to help are perceived as more likeable. Women often report feeling greater pressure to smile, be nice, and find ways to express disagreement in a less direct manner. It is definitely a balancing act that adds to the complexity of situations.

In general, men are viewed as more influential because leadership skills are more consonant with the traditional male gender role than the traditional female gender role. When it comes to leadership behaviors, people allow men more behavioral latitude than they allow women, that is, the band of behaviors that is acceptable for males to demonstrate is wider.

Both Men and Women Internalize Gender Stereotypes

Not only does early socialization encourage males and females to adopt these gender-appropriate behaviors, but also to hold them as personal ideals for themselves. For example, when women managers subscribe to the idea that they should be "nice" most of the time, it may deter them from speaking up to ask for resources they need or from providing reprimands to others. Similarly, male managers are often more uncomfortable with providing negative feedback to women than they are to men, whom they perceive as being tougher and more hardened to receiving criticism. Thus, in each of these examples, stereotypical thinking can arise frequently as a powerful barrier for women in the labyrinth. Often the nice, caring, and friendly qualities that characterize the thinking about women run counter to what we expect from our leaders. Compounding the problem is that there have been fewer women in positions of leadership who can model different varieties of leadership behaviors. The multitude of male role models has provided a greater range of examples of what leadership can be ... for men. The scarcity of female role models in positions of senior leadership has made it more difficult for women to imagine themselves in those roles and to emulate good leadership ... in women.

What Can Managers Do?

The double bind, the double standard, skepticism about competence ... no wonder so many women have been leaving organizations in the past decade. As women's educational attainment and the greater numbers of women in the workforce continue to grow, the social-relational contexts at work will change. As more women move into higher-status positions and excel in formerly male occupations and roles, stereotypical thinking is bound to diminish. These different social-relational contexts at work will provide men and women with experiences of one another that are increasingly distant from the traditional gender stereotypes. Sometimes, raising awareness alone can help people change their perceptions.

You have an important role to play in this process that pushes for changes in stereotypical thinking and gender bias. If you observe other people forming opinions based on stereotypical perceptions, you may wish to speak up about it and assist them in developing greater self-awareness. You also may find that in the course of your managerial responsibilities you can take a proactive role in educating others about the dangers of stereotypical perceptions.

There are some things mentioned in Chapter 4 that yield results that you can put into practice as a manager, without necessarily waiting for your organization to implement a formal program of some kind. These are ensuring fair performance evaluations, spon-soring women's networks, and providing mentoring and coaching to talented women.

Ensuring Fair Performance Evaluations

In order to ensure that your performance evaluations and those of your direct reports are fair, you can examine how stereotypical per-ceptions may be creeping into your evaluations of performance. It is less likely that stereotypes will creep in if your performance manage-ment process contains objective criteria for evaluating performance, such as leadership competencies. The more specific, objective, and measurable the behaviors, the easier it is to be impartial. Even when

Tips
Questions for Your Reflection
• For what behaviors are the men and women on your team rewarded? • How would you characterize the behaviors of the women who succeed? • During performance rating sessions, do you or members of your team question or do they accept the competence of women? • How much evidence do you require in order to reward females with high performance ratings, compensation, and bonuses? • Do you consistently require more time for women to prove themselves, i.e., "just one more assignment" or "another six months" before administering a promotion or bonus to a talented female? What might you do differently to ensure that women are being rewarded fairly?

you do have objective criteria for judging performance, the box provides some questions you can ask yourself.

Women's Networks

Getting to know the talented men and women in one's organization can go a long way toward minimizing stereotypical perceptions. When women and men develop a mutual respect for each other's unique professional capabilities, there is little room for traditional gender stereotypes. Women's networks, mentoring, and coaching provide opportunities for men and women to exchange information about each other's professional expertise. With a minimal amount of investigation, you can probably find resources and authorize some activities in these three areas for the talented women in your group. For example, even if your organization does not sponsor a women's network, you can encourage the interested women in your group or division to start one. Some of the topics discussed by women's networks in other organizations are listed in Chapter 4. There may be local experts on these topics who would be willing to volunteer as guest speakers at these sessions.

Mentoring

With regard to mentoring, you can pave the way for your talented women to approach leaders who could serve as mentors for them. Why not use your influence and make a phone call or two to "put in a good word"? Chances are there are only one or two "degrees of separation" between you and some of the best leaders in your organization. And while we're on the topic, can *you* serve as a mentor to others?

Whether you are male or female, as the discussion in Chapter 3 on mentoring indicates, there are many benefits to you and your organization, not the least of which is enabling cross-gender pairs to learn more about each other's approaches to leadership. Diversified mentoring relationships may also afford you and maybe some of your peers the opportunity to examine your biases and stereotypes in a new light by seeking protégés who may have perspectives very different from your own. Your willingness to be open to fresh ideas and viewpoints may lead you to acquire new knowledge, more empathy, and greater wisdom in your dealings with other people.

Coaching

With regard to finding a good coach for the talented women in your group, asking your colleagues and business associates is a good way to start. Coaches obtain much of their business through referrals, so your human resources professional may know of some. In a book previously written on the topic of executive coaching, I and my co-author, Robert J. Lee, offer suggestions on how to select a coach, the steps in the coaching process, and the importance of the role played by you, the boss, in authorizing the coaching and influencing successful outcomes for talented individuals.[22]

In view of some of the obstacles that women encounter as they move through the labyrinth, managers may need to recognize that certain experiences are especially helpful for women. What are the actions that all managers, both men and women, can take to develop talented women? Are there specific actions that female managers can take to develop talented women, and are there specific actions that male managers can take to develop talented women? Information gleaned from research as well as data from my interviews suggests that there are dual-gender actions, that is, actions that *all* managers, whether male or female, can take to develop talented women, as Figure 5.1 illustrates. In addition, there are also specific things that *male manag-*

Figure 5.1 What managers can do to develop talented women

ers and *female managers* can do to contribute to the development of women.

Dual-Gender Actions

In addition to actions that organizations can take to foster a climate of leadership development and inclusiveness for women and men, there are actions that managers, both men and women, can take to develop talented women. The box overleaf summarizes these actions.

Tips:
What Male and Female Managers Can do to Develop Talented Women

- Become more aware of your gender biases
- Help female managers develop their networks
- Endorse the authority of female leaders
- Send talented women to leadership training programs
- Give women challenging jobs with sufficient support
- Help women avoid "the glass cliff"
- Balance the numbers of men and women on teams

Become More Aware of How Gender Biases Influence Your Decisions

Certainly, your awareness of the problems of holding onto stereotypes is the starting point. Now that you have a better understanding of how stereotypes can inadvertently cloud perception, you can do your best to uncover your own hidden assumptions about the behavior of women and men. If your organization offers a diversity training program that will give you the opportunity to examine your own biases, then make the time for it. In the meantime, there's no substitute for simply doing the mental work yourself, so here are some questions for your own reflection.

Tips:
Questions for Your Reflection

- What assumptions about my direct reports and others do I make based upon their gender?
- What assumptions do I make about men and women that I learned while I was growing up? How do they influence my perceptions currently?
- How do my actions reinforce traditional stereotypes about men and women?
- What examples have I seen recently of the Double Bind, the Double Standard, and Resistance to Women's Leadership? How could I have handled those situations more effectively?
- Do I require more proof of competence from the women in my organization than from the men? If so, how? What might I do differently?

Help Female Managers Develop Their Networks

Women often need help in seeing and using informal organizational networks. This theme was a very common one throughout the interviews. It's quite likely that women and men have different informal networks, paths, and access to the top of your organization. Because women may lack access to powerful individuals in the organization, managers can support talented women by allowing them to expand their networks and build social capital. Women benefit from networking with other women and most certainly with men, who are more likely to occupy more powerful positions. As one interviewee said: "Men often take for granted their access to power. They need to open the door and include women in the power structure."

These actions can take several forms: for example, you can bring a talented woman into your own network both formally and informally by inviting her for lunch or a cup of coffee with you and other colleagues or simply by introducing her to others whenever the opportunity arises. In the words of another executive, "Not only do women not have the natural network that men do, but women are the ones, in many cases, running the show at home, even if they have 'good' husbands. We have greater demands on our time. Being included in meetings with bosses and introduced around during the course of the day would be very helpful. It should be done as a matter of course by our bosses, as opposed to our finding the time to go to lunch or dinner or cocktails on anything like a regular basis."

If your organization sponsors women's networks, encourage participation in networking activities such as events or web-casts. Sometimes these events or activities sponsored by women's networks are of interest not only to women, but to men as well. So you may want to encourage participation by both women and men in your organization. Enabling males to get to know "exceptional," high-achieving women can contribute to a reduction in gender stereotyping as they observe more women in so-called "atypical" roles.

Endorse the Authority of Female Leaders

As we have seen from the research, women leaders face challenges to their competence, and more so from males than from females. Actions that you can take or anything that you can convey to clarify or shed light on the proven competence, experience, knowledge, and skill levels of talented females may help them exert their influence in the organization. As you are aware, wielding influence is critical to the execution of projects and in everyday interactions with others.

When you select women for leadership roles, whether as project team leaders or as functional heads, you may want to inform others about the attributes and qualifications of the female leaders. Stereotypes tend to persist in the absence of a conscious effort to change them. You may want to be ready to respond to the skepticism and resistance by others by figuring out ways of legitimizing the authority of the women selected for those roles. As one general manager of a Fortune 50 high-technology company explained: "Prior to my first assignment in Japan, a friend in Taiwan forwarded to me an email that had been sent by one of the top Japanese executives to his peers. In this email he explained some of my past experiences, praised my achievements, and endorsed me by saying 'She's OK – we can trust her.' It boosted my credibility and helped me be successful in my job."

As mentioned in Chapter 4, organizations are now using technology such as websites that showcase women leaders' accomplishments. You may want to insure that all of the outstanding women leaders in your organization are included in your organization's communication vehicles and that other people in the organization know about their accomplishments.

Send Talented Women to Both Internal and External Training Programs

Women's networks may not be as extensive as men's, but internal and external training programs yield dividends in more than one way. Not only do the participants learn the subject matter, but they expand their opportunities to network. One interviewee mentioned in particular an exercise that had a strong impact on her: "Years ago I was sent to a management assessment program in which one of my assignments was to write a letter explaining where I wanted to be and what I wanted to be doing twenty-five years in the future. I had a hard time figuring out what I saw for myself even two years into the future! My manager at the time criticized me for not knowing what I wanted ten years out. When I mentor people I urge them to figure out what they may want for themselves into the long-term future because it helps to make decisions about today."

Give Women Challenging Job Assignments with Sufficient Support

Some jobs are "gender-typed," that is, thought to be associated with characteristics that are either male or female. For example, upper-level managerial jobs and line jobs have been considered male gender-typed, or *agentic*, whereas middle and lower-level managerial jobs and staff jobs have been considered female gender-typed, or *communal*. The majority of "challenging" jobs are line jobs in which managers must direct and control essential organizational activities with responsibility for profit and loss (P&L). Line jobs also confer more opportunity to ascend into senior leadership. The attributes that are considered necessary to success in line jobs are assertiveness and decisiveness, considered to be more male gender-typed. One of the biggest barriers to advancement for women is the lack of line management experience.[23] The research has shown that women in line positions are more vulnerable to gender-based bias because there is a perceived lack-of-fit between job requirements and attributes of women.[24]

It is important to avoid a scenario in which women are set up to fail. In the words of one of the male managers known for developing women leaders in his organization, "Managers and organizations need to ask how they have prepared women for P&L assignments. They need to make sure that women are going into P&L jobs with a variety of sufficient experiences."

Before assigning a talented woman to a challenging job, you may want to ask some questions to identify more carefully the kinds of challenges or problems inherent in it and the anticipated leadership lessons to be learned from it. In the words of one CEO, "Running your first P&L is very instructive. It's very important that managers develop their people, provide feedback, and assist them to round out their skills."

Steer Clear of the Glass Cliff[25]

Some research indicates that sometimes women candidates are placed in highly risky positions, more often than their male counterparts.

When women are appointed to senior management positions when companies are experiencing financial downturns or declines in performance, they may be more likely than men to find themselves on a "glass cliff," that is, their positions of leadership carry a greater risk of failure. If and when that failure occurs, it is then women rather than men who must face the consequences and receive criticism and blame.

Organizations may offer women these high-risk leadership positions for a variety of reasons. Members of the organization's "in-group" may have already rejected these offers because the individuals in their networks have directed them away from career-threatening jobs and into more secure career opportunities. Women's networks, infrastructure, and resources may be more limited in the organization, so they are not alerted to the "early warnings" about problematic positions or to the safe or "cushy" positions. Another reason may be that these offers are in keeping with the organization's equal opportunity guidelines to appoint women to available positions and the women feel unable to refuse offers, albeit high-risk ones.

To help talented women avoid falling off "the glass cliff," here are some questions for your reflection.

Tips:
Questions for Your Reflection

- What are the challenging "plum" assignments in your organization?
- How are you preparing the talented women in your organization *prior to* taking on the challenging "plum" assignments?
- What types of support and resources such as personnel, increased budget, etc., are you making available to them to enable their success in those assignments?
- What forms of mentoring, coaching, external development programs, or other leadership development resources does your organization make available?
- What specific leaders can you identify who could serve as mentors when an individual woman is assigned to a challenging job?
- How do you know that the job opportunity is challenging but doable? Or is it, in fact, an *impossible* one? What is the likelihood of *anyone* succeeding in the position?

Balance the Numbers of Men and Women on Teams

Being the "token" or solo woman in a group of men places a woman at a disadvantage and increases the risk of stereotypical perceptions. Women exert higher amounts of influence when groups are gender balanced. In fact, group members display more mutual support and agreeableness when more females are present.[26] Both men and women must make attempts to be purposefully inclusive in order to obtain desired business results. Recognizing this, when one senior woman executive walked into a meeting and found herself to be the only woman on a new business team, she humorously quipped to her male colleagues, "Hey, we need more chicks in the room!" She then proceeded to explain to them why, from a business perspective, it was advantageous to have more women on the team. They agreed and added several more women to the group.

Actions by Men

One of the interviewees, a male vice president of a large Fortune 50 company, has been known as a manager who recruits and develops capable women. He has no dearth of talented candidates for positions in his organization. As he explains: "I have had an easier time understanding women because I have had the experience of watching my wife's turmoil in trying to integrate her career with our family. Many women leave the workplace because we don't create the right environment. I try to create an environment for people to feel comfortable, speeding up or slowing down their careers as their situation requires. So I try to have open dialogues with direct reports so that I understand their situations and what they would like to do. What I do now, I couldn't have done twenty years ago at age thirty because I didn't have the life experience. Maybe if I had had a book, I would have learned earlier!"

Thanks to this manager, and to the others who shared their ideas for this book, you now know that there are three things that men in particular can do to contribute to the development of the women with whom they work. They are summarized in the box overleaf.

Tips:

What Male Managers Can Do to Develop Talented Women

- Ask questions to understand the perspective of women
- Overcome the reluctance to provide women with feedback about their performance
- Champion women's leadership development

Ask Questions to Understand the Perspective of Women

As you have seen, when assumptions are made based on female stereotypes, erroneous judgments may result. It is simply good business practice for managers to understand the situation faced by each direct report in order to make wiser decisions and to avoid losing talent. As one interviewee noted, "Male managers should take the time to find out more about the people who work for them. They need to know what makes talented women tick, what their needs are, and how to accommodate them in order to retain them." In the words of one female interviewee with advanced degrees in engineering and manufacturing, "The question is if men can show some vulnerability and be approachable. The outcome will be that more women will ask them questions and be open with them." One general manager recounted her experience with one of her male bosses: "I remember how a number of years ago there was a job located in a different country that was perfect for me. I had all the correct experience ... but I wasn't picked for it. I was so disappointed. One day a short time later, when one of the vice presidents took me to lunch, I finally asked him why I didn't get the job. He replied, 'I didn't know you wanted the job. I thought you had kids, and that you didn't want to travel or live in another country.'" At that point she was even more astonished than he ... because she didn't have any children and she loved to travel! How much better it would have been if he had made no assumptions and had asked her at the time about her interests.

Learning from this experience, this same female general manager now coaches the male leaders who report to her. "I tell them to make sure you ask questions. When someone tells you they want to be a leader, ask them three things: 1) What does that mean to you? 2) What's the job you want to be in on the day you leave the company?

3) What kinds of job experiences are necessary leading up to that job? Then I encourage them to give their support."

Overcome the Reluctance to Provide Women with Feedback About Their Performance

Managers need to provide feedback of all kinds on a regular basis. It is easier to provide positive feedback, of course, and the interviewees emphasized that women definitely need to hear it. In the words of one vice president of technical and business strategy, "Feedback for a woman is very important. A woman reckons that if you don't say anything, she did a bad job." Said another interviewee, "Women need compliments so they can bloom. They tend to be very self-critical. Managers can help them experience success in a safe environment." In the view of a female vice president of marketing and strategy, "Male managers need to validate women more often because it reduces the women's self-doubt. Believe in them and tell them you believe in them. Send them 'happy-grams' – notes of validation and thanks. These go a long way with women and help relieve the self-doubt. And try to reduce the attacks – women go into cocoons when attacked."

One of the most difficult tasks that managers need to do is to deliver difficult feedback to direct reports. Unlike women, men often receive informal feedback through their conversations with colleagues, mainly other men. Sometimes a friend is enlisted, usually another male, to provide difficult or constructive feedback. However, for a variety of reasons, male managers feel very reluctant to have difficult conversations with women. Sometimes they need to be reminded that most women would rather receive important feedback so they can take corrective action rather than have their careers stall because they never received valuable information to help them improve. As one female interviewee said, "Give women straight talk. It is important for women to hear about the negative reactions of others, as men do."

As you can see from the research on the double bind, women need to find the right balance of *agentic* and *communal* behaviors. For many women, knowing how to blend these behaviors is not easy at all. They can flounder and make mistakes. What may help them in this endeavor is feedback from you and others. Sometimes male managers are reluctant to provide women with feedback because they are not comfortable dealing with the emotions that result in crying behavior ("Oh, no! What will I do if I make her cry?"). Here it may be helpful to realize that crying has been the more socially sanctioned way for females to express unpleasant emotions, in contrast to males, who, from early ages, often receive ridicule for crying. Recognize that as a male, you may well have been admonished as a child not to "make girls cry." In contrast, for many males, anger and expressing emotions through sports have been the more socially sanctioned ways to express emotions. And, whether through sports or social situations, recognize that you are probably more used to dealing with outbursts of male anger.

Although most people try to avoid emotional displays in the workplace, sometimes they do occur. When they occur, here are some things you can do. 1) You can ask if the person wants a break and wait for her to regain control. You need not feel as though you must do something. You can simply listen without becoming defensive or feeling as though you have to do a lot of explaining. Seek to understand, not necessarily to take action immediately. Give your time to listen carefully and understand as fully as possible. 2) For the tears, you may want to keep a box of tissues handy. For the anger (as well as the tears), you may want to offer a ten-minute time-out break or a reschedule of the meeting.

Finally, if your organization offers training in how to deliver performance feedback or how to have difficult conversations with others, sign yourself up for it! You will want to feel more at ease when you provide women with feedback about their performance. As one senior male leader in a Fortune 500 company noted: "We've been successful in putting women in critical, non-traditional roles because we need to give talented executives the opportunity. We give them visibility to senior leaders ... and we also give them real-time feedback."

Champion Women's Leadership Development

Women need to have male "champions" within organizations who will encourage women's leadership development efforts. In the words of one interviewee, "An effective manager encourages females by asking, 'Tell me how I can help you be successful in your role. What are the resources you need?'" As one executive director stated: "Male managers need to open the door and give women opportunities for growth. They need to be cognizant of the additional challenges that women face and make it okay to be female in their department." You may want to look for opportunities to serve as a "champion." Some possible actions are to serve as a speaker at a women's event, getting involved in Diversity and Inclusion initiatives in your organization, and using some of the suggestions in this book to effect change. In the words of one vice president of finance: "Male bosses need to take more risks by giving women bigger assignments earlier. Women always have to bang on doors to say we can do it. Don't be afraid to give us more."

As you think about what more you can do, here are some questions to ask yourself.

Tips:
Questions for Your Reflection

- How can I encourage women's leadership development in my department?
- Who are the male role models in my organization who have helped other women leaders?
- What other male leaders can be recruited as "champions"?
- How can the organizations' Diversity and Inclusion initiatives help with this endeavor?

Actions by Women

There are a number of things that women managers in particular can do to contribute to the development of other women. They are summarized in the box below.

Tips:
What Female Managers Can do to Develop Talented Women

- Share experiences with other women
- Recognize the wide range of diversity among women
- Provide realistic feedback

Share Experiences with Other Women

Women are thirsting to hear the stories of how other women have accomplished what they did and how they have managed to get where they are. Because there are still relatively few women at high levels in organizations, what successful senior leaders have learned can provide other women with examples.

When female managers share their experiences, other women are given ideas about what might work for them. As one interviewee said, "Female managers have an obligation to explain to women how they succeeded. For example, other women were interested in hearing about what it was like to be the first pregnant woman at this level in the company, so I talked about it with them." In the words of one female advertising executive: "Women forget the impact we can have on younger women. We need to be cognizant of what younger women are soaking up."

Recognize the Wide Range of Diversity among Women

As a result of cultural and social experiences, women will have different views of what is possible.[27] Many interviewees mentioned the importance for female managers of being non-judgmental regarding other women whose life experiences, demeanors, and even dress may be different from their own. "Female managers need to be more supportive of different styles," said one interviewee. "They often don't have much tolerance for different styles, but being more flexible would be helpful." Said one female executive vice president: "Women need to do a better job at embracing women's differences." Said another: "Just because one leader is a superwoman doesn't mean that everyone is." And yet another woman executive in advertising said: "Women can be their own worst enemies with their female peers. They need to encourage a collegial atmosphere."

Provide Realistic Feedback

When it comes to giving other women feedback, women have more power than they realize. The interviewees saw the action of women giving feedback to other women as critical to success. As one interviewee said: "Female managers can make themselves available and offer their talented women unbiased, unabridged feedback." Said another: "Women can be honest with each other, especially about appearance. They need not take it personally and can simply hire a coach to help them." Another interviewee noted that some types of feedback are more easily given from one woman to another. "There is a reluctance to talk about physical appearance and presence, but it counts," she said. "Even mentors are reluctant to tell someone that they need better grooming." One female advertising executive said: "Women need to do a better job of embracing differences and be more accepting of each other."

Whether you are a male or female manager, as you think about the actions that you can take to develop talented women, the biographical accounts of women achievers found in Chapter 7 may provide you with further insights about the important role that managers have played in their careers.

Summary

As the demographics change, it is likely that more women will move into senior leadership roles. Managers have an important role to play in this change process and it is important that you examine your own behaviors and biases, take off your blinders, and encourage open dialogue with people in your organization. You can provide talented women with key job experiences to enable them to overcome some of the obstacles and disadvantages related to gender stereotypes that they encounter in the labyrinth. Because leaders must demonstrate a range of leadership competencies and styles to be effective, you and your organization stand to benefit by widening this range of acceptable behaviors. In the next chapter you will get a better understanding of the actions that women can take for their own self-development as leaders.

Chapter 6

What Women Can Do to Develop Themselves

Why include a chapter devoted to what women can do for them-selves? Well, why not? We know that very often change must take place simultaneously on many levels – at the individual, organizational, and societal levels. Women can't expect that managers and organizations will always know the best actions to take at any given point in time. Sometimes it takes dialogue with others and trial and error to arrive at the best solutions for any one individual. So in their quest for survival in the marketplace, women must use the most up-to-date knowledge that science and practice have to offer. As we have seen thus far, science and practice have accumulated sufficient knowledge to offer a rudimentary roadmap for women to use on their journeys. Like the pirates' maps of old that showed the locations of the safe passages as well as the swamps and quicksands, the map can assist women in their quest for achievement (and maybe even buried treasures!). Women must strive to excel in their work and take responsibility for their career advancement. They need to take the necessary actions to improve their self-awareness and self-management, the foundations for effective leadership.

Another reason for including a chapter on what women can do to help themselves and other women is because women must continue to be better at it. One interviewee emphasized the importance for women of being good role models to others: "It's okay for women to acknowledge that they are women because what they bring to the table is wonderful. We have to acknowledge that different styles of leadership and management are beneficial. There is no need for us to develop the bravado that men possess and we don't have to pretend to be like the men we see."

In the past several decades, many women have had the experience of being the only woman to "get to the top" and the journey has often been a lonely one. Under the pressure of representing the entire gender, many women have viewed themselves as solo warriors on a battlefield that admits few of their kind. Viewing their special status as something to be preserved, some women tended to be overly competitive with other women, because in a world that admits few women, their position could be threatened by other female candidates for the job. In the words of a high-ranking male in a major consumer products company: "Over the years I've seen competitiveness between female managers, and it seemed as though they are afraid that they will be surpassed by the direct report. My advice to them is to be less competitive. Understand that when you are leading other women it will be seen as positive."

In discussing the slow growth in the numbers of women in senior management, one senior woman executive joked: "There have been stops and starts. It's not like there has been one group of women focused on the single mission of attaining CEO level. It's not been forty years of an army of women marching forward. Some have been marching off to the left, some have been marching off to the right, and some have been AWOL!"

Fortunately, with the increasing numbers of women and the talent needs of organizations today, this situation is changing. Although there are still many women, particularly those in male-dominated industries, who are still facing the pressure of being the only woman in a meeting or on a task force, more and more women are realizing that the demographics are changing. There are and will continue to be increasing numbers of women in the workforce, an important factor in creating change. As one female vice president from the Baby Boomer generation put it, "Women must see women being successful so they can say 'I can imagine myself being that person.' It's important we break the barriers so they can see a woman doing it."

Blending both the results from the research literature and the interviews for this book, this chapter is addressed to women, so that you may consider taking some of the actions that are described here as you make your way through the labyrinth. Chapters 4 and 5 contain some of the relevant research findings that underlie the suggestions in this chapter, and you may wish to refer back to those chapters to refresh your thinking and place them in context.

Some tips for what women can do are outlined in the box below.

Tips:
What Women Can do to Develop Themselves

- Seek feedback
- Make time for reflection
- Join a women's network
- Ask for what you want
- Combine competence with warmth
- Seek high visibility and line assignments with support
- Find mentors
- Seek external stretch assignments
- Ask for an executive coach
- Attend development programs

The Importance of Seeking Feedback

As the research shows, women do not receive feedback in the informal ways that men do. Most of the actions in this chapter will give you the opportunity to obtain both positive and constructive feedback about yourself, if you are ready and open to it. As one executive director of a national educational program said, "As a woman, you must recognize that people have conversations about your performance. You need to have people who can give you feedback and you need to be able to take it."

It may help you to know that many people hate giving feedback about someone's performance and will go to great lengths to avoid it. Why is giving feedback to others so difficult? When most people get around to admitting it, even in structured situations when feedback is expected, such as a performance appraisal discussion, they are sometimes afraid of offending others and of evoking a strong emotional response. So it is important for you to be able to receive feedback in such a way that others will be willing to give it to you. That will require you to control the display of your emotions such as crying and anger in order to be able to focus on what the person is telling you about your behavior.

You may want to take a proactive approach by telling your manager that you very much want feedback of all kinds – even very tough feedback – and that you promise not to cry. When your managers do give you feedback, thank them – especially if the feedback was negative, and let them know you want more. Set up regular miscellaneous discussions with your managers (to review projects, etc.); these are useful to see if you are on track. These also provide regular opportunities for feedback. In those instances when you receive feedback that is upsetting to you and your emotions get the better of you, you might ask for a brief "time-out" or a rescheduling of the session, to enable you to be open to the feedback. You want to be able to hear what someone is telling you and respond with appreciation for the opportunity to grow. Whether you agree with the feedback or not, you will want to take time to reflect on it afterward and consider ways in which you may make the changes you need to make in order to succeed.

When asked what she currently does to develop herself as a leader, one vice president of a high-tech company said: "I work to understand the impact I have and learn how to improve it, sometimes by trial and error, sometimes from mentors, sometimes from people who work for me, sometimes from my family."

The Importance of Reflection

As you work to improve your self-knowledge, whether you are a seasoned leader or a potential leader, you will want to examine the personal side of leadership. One of the female executives who reported to the CEO of a Fortune 10 company, in which she has worked for twenty-two years, offered her advice to other women: "It's wise to think of your career as a journey, not a destination. When you do get to a certain level, you need to reflect on where you want to go. At the end of each calendar year, I think about where I want to be and look at variables and constraints. Some people have gotten ahead by jumping around and others stay where they are, so you need to assess for yourself what is best. Many men have spouses who will move with them every few years. But you need to know what you are willing to deal with and who you are."

One framework that can help you reflect more, focus your thinking, and connect career issues with leadership development activities is found in the book, *Discovering the Leader in You*.[1] Authors Lee and King create a framework organized around five important topics that may be briefly outlined as follows:

- Changing context and demands: What is the context of your current or potential leadership role?
- Vision: What is your own personal vision and is leadership a part of that vision?
- Values: Are your personal and leadership visions based on your own values?
- Self-awareness: What personal qualities support your work as a leader?
- Balance: Do you have adequate balance and focus in your life?

The practical exercises in *Discovering the Leader in You* will enable you to think about your choices, become more aware of what's important to you, and help you manage your career more actively. The next section of this chapter uses the research findings punctuated with comments from the high-achieving leaders interviewed for the book. It is designed to provide you with ideas to enable you to develop and launch your career, as the rockets in Figure 6.1 illustrate.

What Can Women Do?

Join a Women's Network

This is made easier if your organization has one. If not, you may want to consider simply getting together periodically with a group of other women with whom you can share your experiences. There are many benefits to this activity, but some of the most important aspects of it for your work are that you will learn more about your organization and have people to whom you can turn when you need information. On a more personal level, you may feel less isolated, and learn how other women have managed to be successful and have overcome obstacles in their lives. You may find friends and role models as you make your way through the labyrinth. As one female interviewee noted, "Women need to network with each other. And

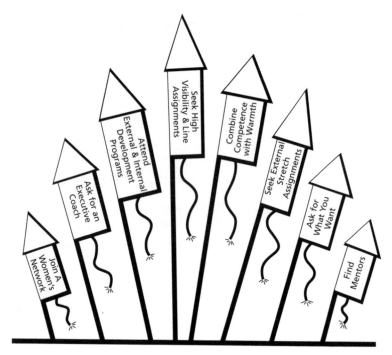

Figure 6.1 What women can do to develop and launch their careers

women managers who are managing females need to be unafraid to show their support of their women direct reports. Women managers must make sure they're not tougher on other women."

Ask For What You Want

Sometimes figuring out what you want is a difficult process. Doing the work required for self-awareness and self-management is not easy. So knowing what you want is the first step. Then you need to ask for it. Many women don't know how to ask for what they want. In their book, *Women Don't Ask*, authors Babcock and Laschever[2] emphasize that in negotiations, women need to be perceived as non-threatening, cooperative, and interested in the needs of others. They cannot be perceived as dominant and overbearing. Sound familiar? Pairing agentic with communal behaviors will allow you to communicate competence and self-confidence and be more successful.

A suggestion for one way to start is given by a senior executive woman who said: "If you have an idea about how things can run better, or how the business can be more successful, let others know. Lots of times we think the improvements are so obvious to others, but they're not. Figure out if there is more responsibility you could take on in the reorganization and offer to do it. You can say 'Here's how I can contribute.' Even if it is not accepted, you get credit for having thought of it."

As one general manager of a Fortune 50 high-technology company said: "Men are targeted in what they want, in fact, the men who report to me tell me the jobs they want. Sometimes I think that men and boys get coaching on what they want the goal to be. When I was growing up, my brothers would claim their positions on teams – I wanted only to be picked and to play! They had mapped out what they were expecting to accomplish. For women to succeed more, they need to be targeted about what they want. But of course, the women don't see enough examples. The men see a lot of role models and it's easy to identify with them. Even successful women struggle to see the jobs they want."

Sometimes women are reluctant to ask for help. Many consider it a sign of weakness or deficiency. Said one university president: "One of the hardest things I had to learn was to ask for help when I needed it. My feeling was that I made this mess and it's up to me to fix it. It took me a long time to figure out that most of the time, it was the organization's problem."

Sometimes merely asking the right question at the right time can lead to results. One senior executive woman told this story: "Years ago when I was passed over for a senior vice president promotion, one of my peers was named, a man who had less experience. Upon hearing the news I collected myself to remain calm and then went in to ask my boss how this happened. He replied, 'Well, he asked for it. He has three kids and he said he needed the promotion.' I stayed unemotional about it, thanked him for the information and left. In two days I was promoted to a senior vice president."

Enhance Your Influence by Combining Competence with Warmth

You may want to refer back to the section on stereotypical behaviors in Chapter 5. If you have received feedback that you are very assertive or that you tend to be intimidating to others, you may want to consider softening your approach by adopting more communal behaviors. You may be able to solicit the help of a friend, peer, or mentor who can observe your behaviors and give you feedback. In the words of one vice president: "Men are able to have a dictatorial style that says 'I'm in charge – listen to me.' When women try to adopt that approach it's not successful."

Seek High Visibility and Line Assignments with Support

See the section in Chapter 3 on Challenging Job Assignments and in Chapter 5 on Give Women Challenging Job Assignments with Sufficient Support. Every organization has its "plum" assignments – those that get your "ticket punched," those that make senior management sit up and take notice. Find out which ones they are in your organization and the type of preparation necessary for success in those positions. As one vice president in a high-tech company related, "When I look back at my career, I realize that getting opportunities starts early. Now when I look at the people in the pipeline in my organization, I encourage my managers to start early to give them leadership assignments. While it is critical that someone not be promoted too early before they are ready, you need to give them opportunities." As one CEO said, "Of course women must do good work to get recognized. Finding a boss who is gender-neutral and gives you opportunities is important. If you don't have a boss who gives you opportunities, find another boss."

You may also need to recognize that you may be embarking on a multi-year process involving successive and incremental roles and responsibilities. As one male executive who has a reputation for developing talented women explained: "I sense that many women think it is a sign of weakness if they have shortcomings. I tell them that it's OK that you don't know everything, but do complement yourself with team members who have abilities different from your own."

Find Mentors

As the section on Mentoring in Chapter 3 explained, having mentors is a necessity in helping you navigate the organization and feel a greater sense of connection and belonging. You will want to have mentors throughout your career. Why? Well, this is a no-brainer. Protégés receive greater compensation, more promotions, and more career mobility than those who do not have mentors.[3] You may want to review the section in Chapter 3 on Mentoring to refresh your knowledge about the value of having both male and female mentors. In the words of one interviewee, "Male mentors are important for women – do not only have female mentors."

Mentors can provide you with career advice, keep you informed about the availability of "plum" assignments, and give you opportunities for visibility with senior management. One senior vice president of a hospitality company told this story about the value of one of her mentors: "I knew I had a safe place to question the status quo. So when I thought I was making less money than all of my male peers, he said 'Yes, absolutely, you are underpaid. You should go ask for more money.' It took six months but I finally got an adjustment. In fact, now I'm even getting a retention bonus."

On a more personal note, mentors may offer friendship and personal support, acceptance, a sense of belonging, and serve as role models for how to function in the organization. Mentors may provide some or all of these functions, which may evolve and vary over time in any given relationship. Many research studies have reported that mentoring can help women overcome barriers to advancement in organizations. Mentors can help to modify stereotypical impressions, reinforce your competence, and use their influence to help you build your base of power in the organization.[4] From your mentoring relationships, you can learn the "ins and outs" of corporate politics, what jobs and pitfalls to avoid, and acquire valuable allies in different parts of the organization. Mentors provide you with career advice and can help you steer away from "glass cliffs." Having multiple mentors who are both internal and external to your organization can be even more advantageous because of the different perspectives, networks, and help they can offer. In the words of one vice president of marketing and strategy for a high-tech company: "Develop a *palette of mentors* from inside and outside your company, different genders, different styles, different organizations – and leverage them to get a complete view of you."

It is important that you make a conscious effort to let your mentors know that you appreciate what they do for you. Many mentors may do things behind the scenes for you that may not be visible to you. When you express your gratitude, they may want to do even more.

Expect that every mentoring relationship you will have in your life will be different. In addition to your informal mentoring relationships, if your organization offers a formal mentoring program and you are eligible for it, sign up!

Seek External Stretch Assignments

These external assignments can take various forms. They include opportunities to sit on a board of directors for a profit or non-profit organization, or possibly serving as a "loaned" executive (usually to a non-profit organization) for a short period of time (usually a year). These afford you the chance to expand your networks, learn new business skills, and obtain a fresh perspective on another topic or discipline. In advance, you may want to find out what opportunities were opened up to those who previously took an external stretch assignment, and do some longer-term planning so that you have an idea of your options following this short stint.

Ask for an Executive Coach

Executive coaching is appropriate and helpful under a variety of circumstances (see Chapters 3 and 4). Many organizations utilize executive coaches for their high-potentials to enable them to accelerate their learning. Perhaps one of your friends or colleagues has benefited from the services of an executive coach. If you are being given a "plum" assignment or have a need to get up to speed very quickly in a challenging assignment, a coach can assist you in the learning.[5] One place to start is to find out how coaching is used in your organization. If your boss and your HR professional agree that coaching would be beneficial, then your HR professional or friends or colleagues may be able to recommend a competent coach to you. As one senior vice president of a global hospitality company said, "Although I have had twenty years of experience in my industry, I meet with a professional coach every other week. It is very helpful as I work to meet the challenges facing me in my present role."

Attend Both Internal and External Development Programs

As the research described in Chapter 5 shows, in comparison with men, women's competence and credibility are challenged more often. Women still need to be concerned about proving their abilities. The opinion of some is that female leaders succeed by performing exceptionally well. Because women's excellent performance can be overlooked, successful women need to make sure that they have honed their skills and abilities. As one executive director noted, "Men are often selected for their ability to fit in, whereas women are selected for their skills." You may want to attend leadership development programs that can provide you with leadership concepts and frameworks that help you understand how to be a more effective leader. Some of these programs allow you to obtain results from multi-rater feedback tools so that you gain a better understanding about how you are perceived by your bosses, direct reports, and peers.

You may also want to obtain some skills training in communication, influencing, and negotiation – all necessary to be able to demonstrate your competence. As one female vice president noted, "In meetings, if the males in the room are ignoring you, you must say 'Excuse me, let me say this again.' Sometimes we women worry that what we say must be perfect, but then the moment has passed and we have missed out on making our point." Women need to assess their skills and avail themselves of the appropriate training and education. You need to feel confidence in your own competence. In her advice to women, one female vice president for finance and administration usually includes: "Don't be afraid to be the expert – to be the authority when you know you have the most information. Take a seat at the table, don't sit in the back of the room. Very effective people read the cues in the room and participate when appropriate. Have the guts to sell your ideas."

Summary

This chapter provides you with some ideas and actions based on research and best practices to help you develop yourself as a leader.

Depending on where you are in your career, some of these ideas may be more useful than others. The important point is that you remain proactive in your leadership development. No matter how seasoned we become, there are always opportunities for us to leverage our strengths and improve our "challenge" areas.

In the next chapter you will learn from several women leaders how they have dealt with the complexities of being both a woman and a leader in today's world.

Part III

Present and Future Leadership

Chapter 7

In the Words of Some of Today's Leaders

This chapter contains stories that were written in retrospect in the words of a diverse group of women leaders. The narratives are firsthand accounts of their leadership experiences during the course of their careers. The names of the actual leaders have been changed to protect confidentiality. At the beginning of each story there is a bit of information telling about the woman leader's situation.

The purpose for including these narratives is to provide you with a better understanding of the variety of experiences that women have encountered in their careers. I asked them to consider the following questions as they wrote their narratives:

- As you look back on your career, what are the two or three defining moments that paved the way for your future success?
- At what point in your career did you decide to take on a leadership role? What were the circumstances?
- What obstacles did you overcome and how did you do so?
- Who else played an important role in your leadership development? What did they do and how did you interact with them?
- In hindsight, was there anything you would do differently?
- What lessons did you learn from these experiences? What advice would you give to women to enable them to advance in leadership positions in their organizations?

Women want to hear each others' stories of how they have managed to get where they are and how they accomplish what they do. In the course of my work as an executive coach I frequently hear men marvel at the accomplishments of individual high-achieving women ("I just don't know how she does it all!"). The narratives you will read in this chapter from the women who graciously agreed to tell their stories may give you some insights into their minds and hearts ... and maybe a bit about how they "do it all."

As you read these stories, one framework you may find useful to apply was developed at The Center for Creative Leadership in Greens-

---

Good to Know:
Five Themes for Understanding the Issues Faced by High-achieving Women

- **Authenticity** is the degree to which you feel you are your true self. Someone who is authentic has a good understanding of her priorities and emotions. It is hard to develop as a leader if you feel you must hide much of who you are, such as your values, styles, and preferences. At different points in life, many women go through some "soul-searching" about who they want to be and what they want to do in the context of the acceptable leadership styles in the organization in which they work.

- **Connection** refers to our human need to be close to other human beings – family, friends, community, and coworkers. Relationships have been seen as a strength of women and connection is important to the development of women leaders. Connection has been associated with the qualities traditionally considered feminine.

- **Agency** refers to the desire to have control over one's life. It is

what motivates us to take initiative, to achieve, and to be self-sufficient. Historically, agency has been associated with the qualities traditionally considered masculine.

- **Wholeness** is the desire to feel complete and integrated as a full human being. A critical task for high-achieving women is to weave various roles and identities into a meaningful whole. Commitment to multiple roles is associated with psychological well-being, life satisfaction, and self-acceptance. The demands of the business world and its insensitivity to caregiving needs make this hard to achieve.

- **Self-clarity** is the ability to understand your own motives and behaviors. Self-clarity allows the individual to grow by enabling her to recognize her values, to show agentic behavior, to live authentically, and to make choices that produce feelings of wholeness.

boro, North Carolina. In their 2002 book, *Standing at the Crossroads: Next Steps for High-Achieving Women*, researchers Ruderman and Ohlott identify five themes that capture the issues faced by high-achieving women as they approach their careers and their lives. These themes are summarized in the box.

As you read these stories, here are a couple of questions for your consideration:

- How do you see these themes reflected in the women's stories in this chapter?
- Whether you are a man or a woman, how do you see these themes playing out in your own life and career?

Alice is a leader of an internationally recognized clinical intervention program at a major university that services schools and communities. She manages a staff of thirty-five faculty members who serve three hundred sites across the United States and its territories. Alice also consults for major organizations in the United States and abroad.

My lifelong experiences have allowed me to master a set of skills that make it possible to manage and/or lead successfully in a number of complex educational and social environments. Scholars have defined leadership as using your skills, behaviors, and attitudes to influence others in accomplishing established goals and objectives.

As I look back at my career, there have been several defining moments that paved my way to my present leadership positions. My leadership journey began when I was a child because I am the oldest of five living children, and as such I was charged with making sure my younger brother and sisters cooperated as directed while my parents were away at work. Thus, I was the oldest of the latch-key kids. This particular experience allowed me to develop and feel responsibility for not only myself but for my siblings. Being the oldest child with supervision responsibilities also allowed me to experience the rewards of ensuring that tasks assigned to us were accomplished in a timely and efficient manner. This early leadership experience taught me how to negotiate and manage the different personalities of people one supervises. Specifically, I learned how to negotiate with individual people to meet their needs while successfully getting the assigned tasks completed.

At age fourteen, I was given specific responsibilities in two of our family businesses. In each, I was charged with organizing and coordinating tasks and monitoring the performance of adults in our employ. This was quite a tall order, as most of the people I monitored were adult men who didn't (often) take too kindly to a young female teenager overseeing and passing judgment on their work. It was through this leadership and management experience that I learned the power of planning, strategizing, and effective communication strategies – specifically how to give explicit directions and offer performance feedback that promoted and facilitated improved performance. Before long, these adult men would seek my feedback and express appreciation for my ability to deliver the praise and the "bad news" about how well they completed a job for our family businesses. I learned to give feedback in a way that was truthful, helpful, but not offensive (most times) – the way my father had described as "in a way that allowed the person to hear it and learn from it." That was tricky. He gave me opportunities to practice so I would not make an enemy, but could make my point! An important skill for any leader!

Another defining moment occurred when my supervising principal tapped me to take on leadership responsibility while I served as a teacher. He and I often disagreed about how things should be done in our school. He attributed our differences to my age and his belief that I was inexperienced and that I had an idealistic view of the world. He was right in some ways. Yet, he always expressed appreciation for my courage and willingness to challenge the way he led the school. I wanted him to think about his autocratic approach and how it differed from my belief in a collaborative approach. He put me in the leadership position because he wanted me to "see how people really functioned in the workplace," he said. What he didn't know was that I already knew how people functioned in a work environment, and that I knew, to some degree, that not all people functioned at the same level at all times. However, I felt that if you could work with them, you could get your supervisees to meet the goals established and to perform at a particular level. So, going into the first leadership position in my career field was really about proving to my supervisor that I didn't have all the answers on effective leadership as a twenty-eight-year-old, but I had more answers than he thought I did! Eventually we learned to work together well, with me appreciating his style and approach to some situations and him learning to appreciate my preference to be more collaborative most of the time.

I became a department chair in my school and that allowed me to draw further on those experiences I had as the oldest child growing up. I learned how the system worked both in the school and in the school district. I used my knowledge, skills, and past experiences to work successfully with the people in my department to accomplish the stated goals, all the while carefully balancing their individual needs with meeting the school and department performance goals. Because of my success in this position, I was encouraged to take on other leadership positions. The success in all positions was based, in large part, on what I had learned as the oldest of five children of working parents and as a teenager who supervised and worked successfully with older adults.

The obstacles that I had to overcome in moving into leadership in my career field revolved around my age, race, and gender. It was apparent to me that because I was moving into leadership at what was perceived to be an early age, I would have challenges. I was supervising people who were considerably older and who did not always value the position I held or the suggestions that I made. They perceived me as being too young and inexperienced to lead a department. That was not necessarily the case. I had come to that position in my career field with some management experience – fifteen years' experience outside of education, so I did know something about managing people and working with them to accomplish goals. I would often surprise my colleagues with solutions I proposed or strategies I used. My approach allowed me to gain credibility with most of the older faculty members.

My other obstacles were race and gender. Most female leaders are perceived as having soft skills and as being more humanistic but not tough enough to weather the more challenging situations that leaders face. Like other females, my opinions or suggestions were sometimes dismissed or disregarded for no apparent reason. I responded to this by reiterating what I proposed and asking why my contributions were rejected. More often than not, I would also make a point of finding the common ground I shared with another person with whom there seemed to be a difference. I would identify the common ground and try to build on that while also looking for other ways that we might collaborate versus taking a confrontational approach. In several instances, it was clear that some people just did not believe a minority could contribute anything of value to a solution or to the profession. What I chose to do in those cases was simply to show that regardless of my gender, race, or age I was (and continue to be) a knowledgeable, skilled, and qualified person. Unfortunately, I still encounter those kinds of persons occasionally and I respond the same way. I want it to be crystal clear that I am not at the table simply because someone decided to give me a position; I am there because I have earned the position and I am there because I am qualified to be there.

In my leadership development journey, there were several people who contributed to my preparation, growth, and success. My early family leadership and business experiences were critical to my development. As I moved into each new position in my career field, I had people who mentored me and often pushed me to do things that perhaps I had not thought about or didn't think that I could do. Every leader needs a strong support system.

Would I want to change how I have taken this leadership journey? No. I have lived out each leadership experience well, meaning I have tried to capture all the experiences fully. Each position had its own gift and challenges.

Lessons I learned along my leadership journey include:

1. There is value in each human interaction. Demonstrate respect and value for each person with whom you work. Learn from each.
2. Being a good model is very important. People study you and what you do speaks loudly.
3. Be committed to your goals but do not mistake your career for your life. Maintain a good balance between work and home.
4. It is so important to be a good leader and a good follower. Surround yourself with people who have skills you lack.
5. Speak in a way that allows people to hear what you have to say. Speak up for yourself when necessary.
6. Learn the power of negotiation, effective communication, networking, managing up, and if you must compromise, compromise up.

Each leadership journey is different, but each requires commitment, sacrifice, a plan and the will to succeed.

Donna is the director of an engineering group for a large aerospace company. She is responsible for program support and process, product and technology research and development, and people development. She manages over a thousand people at numerous sites. She also integrates people, process, tools, and technology across the entire company.

One defining moment occurred for me when I was helping my sixty-year-old mother plan her classes at a local college. I couldn't understand her choice of courses. When she showed me the catalogue requirements, I realized that my mother was not just taking courses for fun, but was trying to earn a degree. She had always wanted to complete college, but took care of her family first. Becoming a widow at thirty-five with five children delayed her plans for continuing education. At that moment, I truly understood what a vision was, since I realized that she saw herself working for her degree.

Another defining moment in my career was when I was put in charge of a department where I had no history or working knowledge. This assignment allowed me to truly look at the job and define what my role as a senior manager was. If the organization had put me in charge of a team where I had had a technical history or where I knew a lot of the people from prior assignments, I would have been occupied with guiding their day-to-day work since I had familiarity with the tasks. Having a team where I had not performed the technical work allowed me to develop skills that would help me in the future. I had to understand at a higher level what the work was; I would never understand the intricate details, but as their manager, this wasn't my responsibility. My job was to understand enough so that I could ensure that people had the resources to do their work. Since I didn't know anyone in the new organization, I had to learn who I could use as advisors as I learned more about the functions of the group. My discovery from this job was that it was my responsibility to provide resources needed to build the workforce and connect them to their future. It moved me from being a micro-managing technical lead to being a manager who could develop a vision, mission, and strategies for a team. At this point, I truly felt like a leader even though I had been a manager for several years.

I also had to improve my communication skills and style so that I could understand this new group and build a relationship with them.

I realized that communication was more than just a back-and-forth exchange; I communicated through my behavior and actions. I tend to brainstorm out loud, and I found myself telling people that I was thinking out loud and not to act on the thoughts immediately. Since I was new to them, they would do what they thought I wanted in order to please me. I realized that they were responding to the position and not the person. This realization helped in subsequent jobs where other teams had the same feelings.

One obstacle that I have faced is the mismatch between my style as a fairly open and outspoken person and a conservative, male-dominated culture. While my colleagues treat me with respect because of my academic background, they sometimes have not listened to my part of the conversation. There are some male colleagues who don't speak to me directly on important issues. They try to change things in my organization by going through others. I would participate in conversations about processes. Even though I was a subject-matter expert in certain areas, they would persist in clinging to old beliefs and traditions when data were presented that indicated that a change was needed. I deal with this through persistence and patience. I would present the data in different formats so that there would be no confusion. I practice active listening and tolerance and try to sort through the issues in one-on-one sessions. This has proven to be successful, although time-consuming. What I realized was that my role was one of being a change agent. The topics where my male colleagues had the most difficulty accepting a different perspective were ones where there were longstanding ways of doing things. Most of theses areas dealt with "people" concerns – criteria for hiring, career development paths, forward planning of a skill, corporate-wide skills planning. I found that I was much more comfortable discussing these than my colleagues and much more comfortable proposing changes. Being a woman allowed me to have a different view of the need to understand the relationships that were needed to perform these activities well.

I also feel that my being Asian also influenced others' and my own behavior. As a typical Asian, I always felt that my work should speak for me. The outcome of my work was what was important and what should be recognized and not me. This was not the environment that existed in the workplace where I was. The typical behavior that I observed was promoting one's self over letting the work speak for the person's capability. Indeed, I have been coached on the need to self-promote. The other interesting aspect of being Asian in a white, male-dominated environment is that people will stereotype groups including Asians and expect certain behaviors from Asians. Non-Asians often believe that all Asians are submissive, quiet, hard-working, and very good in science and math. Because of this, Asians are assigned to certain roles on teams and in the corporation. When someone such as myself (raised in the United States) does not conform to the stereotype, white males do not know how to deal with this. This might be where the dismissive behavior originates.

There were many people who have been important in my leadership development. My family and friends always encouraged me to do my best and not be afraid to step forward as a leader. My late thesis advisor truly encouraged me to think and act beyond what was typical for people in my field. There was a continuous challenge to accomplish more and reach for more and to become the best. He helped me realize that I could achieve more than I ever thought. This attribute has stayed with me, and it has become effortless to think beyond what is normally expected. At work, there are many who have played a role in my leadership development. Some have been excellent mentors and coaches by being frank about the skills that I needed to develop. There were many that influenced me by serving as good role models. I have studied a lot of styles and have copied attributes that have served me well.

I would not have changed anything that I did or that has happened to me. All of my experiences – personal and professional – have helped me to become the person and leader that I am. I find that these experiences and events have all enriched me. The people who have helped me directly or indirectly have become a valuable network, ready to listen, share, and advise.

I would advise other women to identify mentors and learn from them. Initiate appointments with mentors and listen to what they have to offer. As you progress, keep these mentors, but also add new mentors to renew your perspectives and to expand your network. I would also advise other women to be good mentors themselves. We can learn from the next generation and serve as the role models that they need. I would also advise women to take advantage of opportunities outside of work to develop their leadership skills. They should find an organization that resonates with them (a charitable organization, church, board) and volunteer their services. Leadership skills that are developed in this way will serve women well in other areas of their lives. Sometimes, we don't have the opportunities to build certain skills at work. Volunteering for something where you have a passion can help develop these skills. It also allows us to remember to maintain work–life balance.

Be certain to take care of those that you care about. Much has been written about work–life balance. A good leader will look for the right balance for herself and take into consideration the important people in her life. Working hard to attain the right balance for the individual enables her to be at her best at work.

Finally, we have to remember that, as leaders, we should develop visions, have the courage of our convictions, and always, always take care of our people.

Frances is a vice president of strategy for a global IT company, responsible for both technical and business strategic studies and plans. Her direct report team includes six technical and business executives in five world-wide locations. Her prior assignments have included executive roles in manufacturing, development, and quality assurance.

I decided to enter management early in my career, taking over the group in which I worked. At the time it seemed like a really hard decision: all the role models in college and graduate school, and even in my company, were in the strictly technical career path, and management was viewed as a cop-out by the true techies. But I looked in my internal mirror, and realized that I was better as a coach than as a bench scientist, and decided to give it a try at least (well, I didn't really want to work for any of the other manager candidates!). The tradition was that the manager was also the chief engineer, and the expectation was that the manager could do the tasks of the group members as well as they could. After about four years of managing in this manner, I moved to another part of the company. Soon after my arrival, we reorganized the workgroups to be aligned to customer segments. The new workgroup contained many different skills and roles, and I quickly realized that I could not manage as I had before. It was unrealistic to expect the manager to be able to excel in all the roles, and in my own case, none of the roles was in my own area of expertise. It also occurred to me that the old way of managing could undermine the empowerment of the employees . . . that if the manager could always "fix a mistake" or worse yet "edit the work just for style," then the employee might not bother to do the final polish.

I decided to consciously change my management style, and met with my workgroup to explain why and how. "I cannot do any of your jobs as well as you can, so you need to be fully responsible for the final product. What I can do is to serve as a sounding board, a liaison between you and with other groups, a logic check on your overall approach, and an advocate for you." I was astonished at the fruit of this change. Morale increased as people took more pride in their work. Customer satisfaction increased. Other teams noticed, and my folks were given opportunities for advancement in other areas. And instead of fretting over every detail, I could keep my eye on the critical deadlines and overall strategy, confident that my folks could handle the day-to-day requirements.

This experience changed forever my management approach, and I firmly believe that this management style has enabled me to better develop leaders on my teams and to move to different areas of my company, with fewer fears about not being a "content area expert." When I enter a new area (and in some cases, this has meant moves into areas where I have literally *no* technical background and little personal network), I am very blunt with my team: "I am not here to be the expert. You are the experts. I am here to help make your great technical work have greater impact on our company and client success." There is always some shock and horror in their faces. And then they never look back again, as the same transformational benefits emerge.

The other defining experience came several years later, when I was promoted to my first executive position, responsible for a development team dispersed across the world. In particular, one large laboratory was located in Japan, and headed by the most senior technical "fellow" in the country. Unfortunately, the development strategy his laboratory was following was neither affordable financially, nor was it enabling the local manufacturing team to be successful. The manufacturing personnel were not even allowed access to the laboratory buildings! There was also a heritage of distrust of the American "home office" owing to competition between a US lab and the Japanese lab over technology choices. For a younger American female to compel this Japanese shogun to change his plans was a daunting task to say the least.

Ironically, help came from two very unexpected quarters. The first was that the manufacturing management desperately needed help from development, and were willing to take the risk to help me. The second: the week before my trip to Japan, where we would spend five days redoing the development strategy and plans, I conducted a conference call with both development and manufacturing senior management (all older than me, all male). The call was in the evening, U.S. time, to enable a mid-morning time in Japan. I explained the purpose for my upcoming trip. The phone was completely silent. Suddenly my youngest son, at that time two years old, wandered into my home office and said "Why?" loudly enough to be heard across the world. The manufacturing lab manager chuckled, and said, "Well, that was my question too." The phone erupted in laughter ... and we were a team from that moment forward. The lesson? Sometimes we assume that we have to be so professional that we aren't fully human ... and it is as humans that we really do our best work.

I have had the opportunity to work for some great managers in my career, who helped me learn how to lead. The best of them combined a real warmth as humans, which built strong teams and shared values and goals; an insistence on data-based rather than opinion-based decision making; an attention to detail; and a constant search for external sources of information to avoid "group think." Of those managers, the one I most admire, although he is no longer with my company, was the one for whom I worked the hardest, and the one with whom I laughed the most. I think that is not an accident. He was absolutely candid (but never rude) in everything he did. If he thought you were doing a good job, he would praise you in public. If he thought you had just been an idiot ... you can guess the rest! That was certainly a motivation to do my best work! He was an extraordinarily high energy person: he managed to play more sports, read more books, watch more movies, absorb and retain more facts than his whole staff combined ... and you never knew which of these hobbies would come through as an analogy in the business world. "Don't fold like a cheap suit" he would say when a tough negotiation was in front of us. "Let's not argue about who had the chicken salad sandwich" when we were embroiled in internal accounting arguments and losing sight of the customer's needs. I still use a bunch of his quotes. He also genuinely thought about the workers on our manufacturing floors, and how to help them understand the bigger picture and feel genuinely appreciated for their dedication.

If I reflect on my career path thus far, while it sounds impossible, I am not sure I would change a thing. I learned, over the course of time, that I need to be in charge of my own priorities and decisions, and that I need to define what success looks like for me, in terms of work–life balance. I also learned that I am my most successful when I am most authentically me.

Rebecca is Vice Chancellor for Student Affairs at a public technologically oriented university with about six thousand students in the Midwest. She is one of four vice chancellors comprising the chancellor's executive cabinet and oversees all programs and services that touch the lives of students outside the classroom. This includes intercollegiate and intramural athletics, career services, counseling, health services, leadership and cultural programs, residence halls, Greek housing, student organizations, student union, performing arts theater, university golf course, food service, and the bookstore.

I have always had an interest in leadership and management and been willing to take on new tasks, roles, and challenges that were not necessarily along the path I had laid out. Taking responsibility for a campus-wide Freshmen Orientation Program helped build my credibility and leadership skills in ways I had not envisioned. As a young professional on a male-dominated campus, I trained, supervised, and coordinated activities that included several tenured professors and administrators. Age and gender were challenges early in my career, because of perceptions and biases in others. Building credibility and doing a good job were essential for my future success as a professional and leader on campus.

As chair of the campus Retention Committee I was able to get faculty and administrators to take a serious look at campus climate and issues related to student success and graduation. Furthermore, we were able to create some solutions that have led to significant increases in student enrollment and graduation rates. Leading this effort, which was not part of my regular job description, further enhanced my credibility and expanded my influence on campus. These two experiences helped pave the way for future leadership opportunities on campus.

I was promoted to Assistant Director early in my career over an older colleague who had been hoping for the position for a long time. We had an open and direct conversation about my promotion and what it meant to him and our relationship. A few years later when I became Director, he took on some special projects and served as consultant for me when considering changes and new initiatives in the department. Before his retirement he told people that I was the best boss he ever had because I was interested in his perspective and helped promote his professional development. In many ways he helped me learn to be a good leader. Observing reactions, listening to ideas and feelings, and responding to concerns expressed by professionals are important to being an effective boss and leader.

A challenge I faced a few years later was hiring, training, and supervising new professionals, as I had become accustomed to supervising experienced, senior-level professionals. New professionals need considerably more direction and specific feedback on a regular basis, whereas the senior-level professionals I have supervised liked to be consulted and appreciated autonomy. Although every employee is unique in their personal preferences and needs for professional guidance and feedback, all employees want to feel valued and appreciated by their boss.

I try to look for ways to maximize the use of individual talents to meet organizational needs. Sometimes you can find an immediate opportunity and other times you have to work to create future possibilities. Limited financial resources are always a challenge working in a public university. During a major financial crisis few years ago we had to cut programs, close some units, and lay off employees. By talking with employees in a unit that was being closed, I discovered that one employee wanted a flexible clerical position for two years until she retired, so we were able to use her as a floater for vacations and vacancies for those next two years. Another employee was completing a degree in rehabilitation counseling, so she was promoted to a new position where we had a growing need for service. As Disability Support Services Advisor she has developed an entire new program for the campus.

This same budget crisis led to elimination of two non-spectator intercollegiate athletic teams. Athletics had been financially stretched for several years so we had part-time coaches in several sports and those teams ranked at the bottom of our athletic conference. By eliminating two sports, we were able to pool our financial resources to hire full-time coaches for all of our other intercollegiate athletic teams. We now have athletic teams that are in championship play-offs and athletes who achieve national recognition. However, this cut caused a lot of grief as a few individuals were very upset by the decision to eliminate the men's golf team. They complained vehemently via the media, but never came forward with any financial support to help keep the golf team. Leadership requires decision making, which means you have to make decisions people do not like. That is one of the challenges of being a leader.

As I have moved up the leadership ladder, dealing with demands for visibility and increasing levels of public scrutiny have been challenges for me. Attending many extra events is exhausting because of the lack of downtime. Leaders become targets for gossip and other people's dissatisfaction with their jobs, careers, and lives. Even with limited information, people often have opinions and critiques of decisions which they openly share. The media seems to thrive on negative things rather than successes and people tend to talk about what leaders do. Since I live in a small town, sometimes I feel like I live in a fishbowl. Being healthy and rested is important for me to deal with some of the stress associated with leadership expectations and roles.

I have always valued the importance of building good relationships with colleagues, supervisors, and subordinates. There is also the need to maintain good boundaries to be an effective supervisor, so the higher you go up the leadership ladder, the more you have to work at building your own support system outside your work environment. Mentors, friends, and colleagues have played a significant role in my professional development and success. Being able to talk with people who do not work for you or with you allows you to step back and get a perspective on what is going on in the organization and the profession. Professional organizations can provide training, networking, and colleagues who appreciate your challenges.

Mentors have been important throughout my career. My mentors have included faculty members, experienced colleagues in my professional organizations, bosses, family members, and friends. Only a couple of my mentors have been women. My late mother-in-law was an early and steady source of inspiration in my career. She encouraged me to set challenging goals, taught me to look for resources to pursue my goals, was there to console through challenging times, and celebrated my career successes. It gave me great joy to experience her mentoring and to listen to the stories of other women for whom she had been a mentor. Mentoring young women up the career ladder is a legacy I want to continue in her honor as a boss and in my professional organizations.

I have been fortunate to work for some good leaders who also provided informal mentoring. Early in my career some of my bosses helped prepare me for my next career step. We never talked about it as mentoring, but I have come to recognize it as informal mentoring. These leaders stand out because I have had bosses who were difficult, demanding, and competitive. It was almost like they were trying to impede my career advancement.

Although mentors become scarce as you move up the leadership ladder, I have worked for two chief executive officers who were role models and served as informal mentors. Both demonstrated the value of being a good boss and developing the people who work for you, but in different ways. One supported my professional and leadership development by encouraging me to attend the Harvard Institute for Educational Management, to stay active in my professional organizations and consulting activities, and to run for president of my national professional organization. Although these organizations were related to leadership and consulting psychology rather than specifically to my job as Vice Chancellor for Student Affairs, maintaining the ties increased my job satisfaction, enhanced my leadership effectiveness, and provided some recognition for my university. My other boss demonstrated effective leadership by actively building relationships with faculty, staff, and community members, and communicating with the campus community on a regular basis about change initiatives and progress at the university. He sought additional salary increases for his executive team members to make our salaries commensurate with our peers in the university system and directly told each of us we were important for the success of the university.

I think the balancing act is a challenge for most leaders because of the constant shifts and demands. You have to maintain balance between successfully completing what is required in your current job, finding new challenges, providing service to organizations, spending time with family and friends, and taking care of yourself. Probably one of the hardest things is being able to let go of roles to take on new ones. I have been involved in professional organizations and consulting activities for several years, but after finishing a three-year term in the presidential rotation of my organization I decided to step back and let others take over. Some board members tried to keep me tied in, but I had to let go of something that had been meaningful for several years in order to explore new things. I also worked with a coach training group for a few years, but it became more taxing and challenging on top of my growing job. At one point I realized that I was taking significant vacation time to do a project that had lost its luster for me. It was the greatest thing at an earlier point in my career when I had the opportunity to work with the visionary founder, but my job had grown tremendously and the people I worked with on the project had changed.

In hindsight, I wish I had spent more time cultivating a support system throughout my life and career. Although I continued to exercise to maintain my energy and sanity, I spent many years focusing on building my career and raising my family. Once my children were launched to college it was apparent that I did not expend enough time and energy on building my own support system. Now that my children have professional careers, I am spending more time on recreation and relationships that give me more energy. I enjoy yoga, Pilates, and weight lifting for personal renewal and am learning to play golf. There is a real excitement associated with learning a new sport and meeting new friends/colleagues whom I may have never met without the Executive Women's Golf Association. I am thankful that a good friend encouraged me to pursue this new passion. It will even be helpful at work to play in university and professional association golf scrambles and tournaments.

> Sara is currently a Vice President of Global Procurement for a global consumer products company with responsibility for establishing strategies that deliver consistency in quality, assurance of supply, and predictable economics in key markets around the globe. She has a direct report team consisting of nine procurement professionals who work closely with the different business units worldwide.

Growing up in an Asian family, my siblings and I were taught to excel in whatever we did and to choose a career where we could stand on our own two feet. My father defined such a career as one of three: a doctor, a lawyer, or a CPA (certified public accountant). Although my sister opted to be a stay-at-home mom to her three children, my brother became a lawyer and I the CPA.

After graduating with a B.S. in Accounting I began my career in the Big Eight (now the Big Four) and soon learned about hard work and discipline, particularly during the "busy season" when an average day spanned fourteen hours a day, seven days a week for three to four weeks! During my seven years with the accounting firm I had many valuable experiences, but the one that I look upon as one of my greatest growing experiences was one in which I had to trust in myself and in my capabilities despite having dropped the ball on a recent assignment. Regaining my confidence was only part of the challenge. The greater challenge was in convincing the Partner on the engagement to give me a second chance to prove my managerial capabilities on a highly visible assignment. It was a critical time in my career with the firm as I was in line for a promotion to Manager. I knew that if I could deliver on this assignment I would be a shoo-in for the promotion to Manager.

The assignment proved to be a huge success in the eyes of the client, the Partner and my team. A month later I was promoted to Audit Manager. It was sometime later that I learned that it was that same Partner who had pushed the hardest for my promotion to Manager. From this experience I learned that failure could also be a critical experience in shaping one's career path. The key is to learn from the mistakes, but not to dwell on them. I am forever grateful to that Partner for trusting in me to bounce back and to successfully oversee the assignment.

Two years later I made the decision to leave public accounting and pursue a career in accounting with a consumer products company. Although my salary increase would have taken me at least two to three years to achieve if I had stayed in public accounting, it was a bit of an ego blow to go from a Manager title to a Senior Financial Analyst. I knew that my career move would eventually pay off, but those first few months were not easy. I knew that I could quickly earn the trust and confidence of my boss by being focused and committed and seeking out opportunities to demonstrate my skills. Within nine months I was promoted to a supervisor role and a year later I was the manager of the team. It was in this role that I had my first daughter and had to quickly learn the art of juggling. After only nine weeks of maternity leave I returned to work and my daughter began daycare. Although I was convinced that this was the right thing for her and for me, the guilt was overwhelming at first. I remember many times crying as I drove my commute to the office, ducking quickly in the ladies room when I arrived to fix my make-up. Luckily my daughter quickly adjusted to daycare and I was able to focus back on my job.

Within six months of returning from maternity leave my boss called me into his office to have a career discussion. I had been in the manager role about a year and was ready and excited to move out to a division accounting role. This had been the career path of the previous managers in the department. My boss began the conversation by describing what he saw as my future potential in the company. I was thrilled inside as he described my leadership potential and knew that he had a career plan that he was about to share. I sat at the edge of my chair as he described a job opportunity that had surfaced in a department called Global Procurement that he felt sure was meant for me. I remember being confused and shocked by what I was hearing. After all, accounting was my passion. Accounting was where I had had always envisioned my future as I moved up the corporate ladder. I tried to listen as my boss described the role and his rationale for moving me into another function. He believed firmly that a couple years' exposure to an Operations-type role would serve as a tremendous broadening experience. He described his plan to bring me back into accounting after three years as a director. The idea of becoming a director in three years thrilled me, but leaving accounting scared me to death.

After much discussion with my boss, my spouse, and myself I agreed to meet with some of the leaders of Global Procurement to get an understanding of the function and the specific role. It was in these meetings that it became clear to me that such a move, while more risky than staying in Accounting, would clearly broaden my exposure and my experiences. I decided to make the move with a clear plan to come back to my comfort zone within three years. That was twelve years ago … and I have never looked back! My journey in Global Procurement has been both rewarding and fulfilling. I have been very fortunate to work with highly motivated, highly skilled professionals, including many managers who have provided the coaching and mentoring that have shaped my career.

As I think back on the one or two experiences that have stood out in my mind as important lessons, one that stands out is one in which I learned to always be true to myself, to always uphold what was important to me. At the time, I had been a director for about two years and had recently assumed a new role in which I reported directly to the Chief Procurement Officer. In addition, I was now officially on the Leadership Team of Global Procurement. This was a huge honor for me as it meant I was part of the "inner circle" of Global Procurement. In addition, I was the only woman on the Leadership Team comprised of approximately eighteen to twenty executives. I had been in my role for about six months when I received an invitation to attend a Leadership Meeting in Key West from May 12 through May 14. The reason I remember these dates so vividly is because they presented a major personal conflict for me. May 13 was my second child's birthday. For days I anguished over what to do, as birthdays for me have always been special. No matter what the age, a birthday was a day of celebration. I had always taken a day off for my children's birthdays. I sought the advice of my parents and my friends. It seemed that everyone I talked to felt that there was no issue. Of course I had to go to the Leadership Meeting; after all, birthdays come every year. We could celebrate her birthday in advance of my departure. She would not even remember that Mom wasn't there for her actual day. It wasn't until I was speaking with a girlfriend, who helped me realize that only I could answer the question of what was the right thing to do for me, that I knew what I needed to do. That evening I left a voicemail message for the Chief Procurement Officer letting him know that owing to a personal conflict I would not be able to attend the Leadership Meeting. After hanging up the phone I remember thinking yes, I had done the right thing … for me. The next morning I received a message back from the Chief Procurement Officer letting me know he had received my message, that he understood that personal conflicts do come up from time to time, and that I would be missed. To this day no one has asked me for an explanation as to why I was unable to attend the Leadership Meeting in Florida. My personal decision to not attend the meeting has never impacted my career path.

A year and a half later I was promoted to Vice President. It was in this role that I was faced with my greatest personal challenge. A year ago my husband of fifteen years and I decided to get a divorce.

Although I was mentally prepared for being a single Mom, it meant making significant changes to my work schedule and my travel schedule as my children were eleven and eight at the time and clearly needed a parent at home. I knew what I needed to do. I spent two weeks thinking through how to best position it to my boss. I was looking to continue in the same role with the same level of responsibility, but I needed to work from home before and after school five days a week. Although work–life balance was increasingly discussed within the organization, this level of flexibility was unprecedented. The day came for me to make my request. I began the conversation with "the what" and then quickly moved to "the why." I ended my request with a proposal to trial my flexible work schedule for a thirty-day period at which time he and I would touch base to review what was working and what was not. The discussion lasted for less than five minutes with an unquestionable level of support from my boss. It has been six months since I began this flexible arrangement and I have never been happier. I fully expected that my children would benefit from this, both academically and personally, but I could never have imagined the self-satisfaction that I feel being an integral part of their everyday lives while still maintaining the level of responsibility that I have in my job. I believe that I have found the perfect work–life balance for what I and my family need while continuing to meet the needs of the organization.

As I reflect on my twenty-two years in the workforce, I feel very fortunate to have had the experiences that I have had. Hard work, determination, and being true to self have all been key factors in my journey thus far.

Chapter 8

What Does the Future Hold?

As many of you know, the best way to meet the needs for talent in your organization will be by hiring the best people you can find in the first place. In the future, a large percentage of them will be women. That fact will affect everyone mentioned in the book's introduction: women, men, bosses of women, CEOs, HR executives and professionals, coaches, and researchers. Each of you will find different aspects of this chapter appealing and applicable to your situation.

This is both an exciting and perplexing time for women. It is exciting because there are many opportunities for new jobs in the workplace. It is perplexing because, until now, the pace of change has been occurring at different rates at individual, organizational, and societal levels. At the individual level, women's educational attainment is surpassing those of men. Women are preparing themselves for high-level jobs with increased amounts of responsibility and compensation. Given the numbers, more women will be in the workforce; and by sheer numbers it is likely that many of them will fill leadership roles.

Do you suppose that this was what the organizers of America's first Women's Rights Convention in Seneca Falls, New York had in mind in 1848? The organizers, among them Elizabeth Cady Stanton, issued a long list of grievances from disenfranchisement to unfair child custody laws. The convention participants resolved to demand equality. The outcome was met with derision by the newspapers. The American government finally passed legislation in 1920 granting women the right to vote and much later in the 1960s prohibiting discrimination in the workplace. Since the Seneca Falls convention, it has taken roughly a hundred and sixty years and six generations of women and men to deal with the challenge to use their combined talents to work and live together. One way to parse this challenge is look at what still needs to be done at three levels: the individual, organizational, and societal levels.

Changes at the Individual, Organizational and Societal Levels

The *pace* of change is different at the individual, organizational, and societal levels. Therein lies part of the problem.

Change at the Individual Level

At the level of the individual, the passage of legislation in the twentieth century made formal education more available to women and they have opted to take it. Education has always been a way of "moving up" in America. As the non-dominant group, women have been using individual survival mechanisms to their advantage. Unfortunately, they have encountered organizational and societal barriers that have slowed their progress. Since the 1970s, we have seen increasing numbers of women spilling out of our educational institutions, ready and prepared for work that will sustain them for lifelong careers. In the words of one university dean: "I have twin daughters and I struggle with what I tell them. I show them what I do for the women I mentor and tell them to arrange things so that they have options." Organizations and the society at large have been slower to adapt to the increased numbers and expectations of this "less dominant" segment of society.

Change at the individual level has been all about options, and women have more of them than ever before in history. Within two generations, women have the freedom to make unprecedented choices. Young women now have options concerning what schools to attend, what sports to play, what careers to pursue. Women can choose when, how, and whether to bear children. Economic dependence on men is no longer a necessity. These options have provided women the opportunity to use their brains and make scientific and other professional contributions as never before.[1]

Change at the Organizational Level

Researchers' own experiences in the workplace have led them to investigate the difficulties in career advancement that they themselves were encountering. By the 1980s, researchers had named the barrier "the glass ceiling."[2] By 2007, the numerous subtle barriers were recognized as a "labyrinth."[3] As explained in Chapter 5, stereotypical perceptions, the double bind, and the double standard are some of the obstacles in the labyrinth that have slowed the progress of women. In the face of these barriers, many women have been choosing to opt out, that is, to leave organizations. Given the talent needs of the future, this trend may well have deleterious results for organizations.

During the past decade, there has been much written about the numbers of women leaving organizations that they perceive as unfriendly to them.[4,5] Early in 2004, the Center for Work–Life Policy formed a private sector, multi-year task force called "The Hidden Brain Drain: Women and Minorities as Unrealized Assets" to understand the scope of the opt-out phenomenon. For many women in the study, the decision to leave their organizations was fraught with conflict. After investing heavily in their education and training and spending years building the skills necessary for successful careers, women risk much by "off-ramping." Women lose an average of 37% of their earning power when they spend three or more years out of the workforce.[6]

When asked why women quit organizations, the interviewees for this book were unanimous in their answers to this question – although each expressed it a bit differently. In the words of one interviewee with engineering degrees: "I have friends who left when they thought that the leadership didn't have a vision. Women leave because they don't have the supports or it's too difficult to get the job done because there's no daycare." Women ask themselves, "Am I being heard? Why am I here if no one is paying attention to me?" In the words of a senior vice president in a leading global company in the hospitality industry, "Women make choices about their time and priorities. They have responsibilities at home with their husbands, children, and aging parents. Women do everything; it is the biggest challenge. The majority of my male colleagues have wives who don't work. Women get to a point and say, 'Is it worth it?'"

When advancement has been blocked for women in organizations, many women have become entrepreneurs. Opting out of organizations may be the result of women's dual realization that promotions will be scarce and that their increased responsibility for caretaking needs often require a career adjustment.[7] The section in Chapter 4 on Career Redesign offers some ideas for organizations to consider as they design work for the future. It makes sense for organizations to design work so that both Gen X and Gen Y men and women can return from caretaking periods without being marginalized for the many years remaining in their careers. Clearly, change needs to occur more rapidly at the organizational level. Offering flexible work arrangements (FWAs) without a supportive culture will not be enough. It is important for organizations to create supportive work–life cultures so that men and women can have the flexibility they need to have lives beyond work.

The opt-out phenomenon may be having exactly the opposite effect of what individuals and organizations now need. As the *Catalyst's* 2004 *Bottom Line* study showed, the presence of women leaders has a positive effect on organizations' bottom line. Therefore, increasing the pool of talented women available to work in organizations is desirable. Depending on your situation, you may experience this in a variety of ways. For women, you may desire to be in a senior leadership role and would like to see more women as role models and colleagues. For men, you may enjoy the interactions with female bosses, direct reports, and colleagues who may have a point of view and perspective on the world that is different than your own. For CEOs and HR executives, you may be interested in attracting and retaining the best talent available in the workforce. You may also obtain personal satisfaction in knowing that once you have succeeded in hiring these women and men, you can offer an environment that enables them to grow in their knowledge, skills, and abilities and then rewards them fairly for their contributions. *All of you* certainly have the desire to achieve business results and be proud of the organization for which you work.

Change at the Societal Level

The world seems to be shrinking more and more each day. The news reports help us realize how we are all touched by the effects of global climate changes, the world economy, and natural disasters such as earthquakes, floods, and tsunamis. We are also faced with news information about how different societies deal with situations common to the human condition: the availability of honest work, the health and well-being of families, and the care of children and elderly (death and taxes are excluded from this discussion!). For those of you interested in how change at the societal level may affect individuals and organizations, this section will contain some ideas for you.

The future of women's leadership cannot just rest on the ambitions of a segment of the female population or on the desire for organizations to create wealth and do the right thing. In fact, one can argue that little change would have occurred at all without the legislative and public policy initiatives that started to gather momentum in 1848. As Rhode and Kellerman suggest in their 2007 book, *Women and Leadership*,[8] there is much to be done in the areas of government regulation and public policy, proportional representation, professional and public interest organizations, and educational institutions.

In the area of government regulation and public policy, women's representation could be strengthened by expanding enforcement of equal employment opportunity requirements and anti-discrimination enforcement. Policies related to child care, elder care, parental leave may need revision to increase women's labor force participation, increase males' caregiving involvement, and reducing work–family conflicts.

Clearly, changes in public policy will be successful only if they rest on a solid foundation of research. We need studies that provide evidence linking work–family policies and practices to employee performance outcomes. What criteria are best to use to evaluate the success of work–family practices? Which work–family practices and policies best function as organizational "best practices"? There are many unanswered questions about how work–family practices and policies can best be integrated into the overall business strategy and human resources practices of organizations.[9]

Proportional representation has been advancing in a number of countries that employ mandatory quotas for women in public office. This is a complex issue, but finding ways to increase the gender balance in the U.S. political system needs to be a priority. Professional and public interest organizations can prepare women for leadership and provide more training, mentoring, and educational programs on diversity-related issues and can lobby for public policy reforms.

In a similar vein, educational institutions such as universities and business schools could model the strategies associated with diversity by including more diversity-related issues in core curricula. They should offer courses in the development of women's leadership and provide support for joint academic–practitioner research projects. Some ideas for such projects are provided in the next section.

Questions for Practitioners and Researchers

This section addresses some possible future directions for joint problem solving to be done by researchers and practitioners. As you have read this book, you may have pondered some questions with the potential to affect us all at the individual, organizational, and societal levels. The broad range of topics in the following questions reflect the subject matter of the book and has implications for the areas of organizational culture, gender roles, leadership and team development, work–life integration, demographics, ethics, and educational training. Some of the questions even have an international focus and deal specifically with female leadership worldwide. This reflects a point made in the Preface that many of the ideas in this book may transcend culture and country and spark the interest of others across the globe.

You are invited to add your own questions to the list offered here of some important questions in need of answers by men and women in organizations today:

- What are the optimal conditions that foster women's leadership in organizations? What are the features of the culture that enable women to thrive?
- What are the changes taking place in the values and attitudes of the workforce? Are the so-called generational differences between the Boomers, Gen X, and Gen Y truly valid? Either way, what are the implications for women's leadership?
- What have been the effects of the following types of programs on the development and advancement of women leaders: mentoring programs, women's networking groups, executive coaching?

- How does the increase in flexibility in gender roles influence the development of leadership skills in the "emotional competency" cluster such as relationship building, self-awareness, conflict management, and teamwork and collaboration?
- How do the dynamics of a team composed of a majority of female members compare with a team composed of a majority of male members? What changes occur on a team as the composition slowly changes from mostly male to mostly female?
- What are the legislative outcomes for governing bodies (boards of directors, parliaments, congresses, etc.) that are comprised of 40% females?
- How do managers' stereotypes about male gender roles affect male direct reports? How does stereotypical thinking disadvantage not only women, but men as well? How might stereotypes place limitations on the kinds of experiences that younger generations of males seek, the very experiences that could influence their ability to become great leaders?
- How can both women and men achieve greater career–life integration in today's organizations? What new processes can be explored and results measured?
- If research shows that women are less tolerant of unethical behavior, will the increased prevalence of women in leadership roles decrease fraud in top management?
- What are the best practices that foster leadership development at earlier periods in human development? What might be done at the grade school or high school levels to encourage leadership in girls? How might researchers measure the success of these practices?
- What are the questions to be explored by emerging countries as more women worldwide assume leadership roles? How does the culture assist or hinder female leadership?
- How do some of the ideas, questions, and suggestions in this book pertain to women and men internationally? In multinational companies? In different countries?
- Women in the United States are ahead of other countries in education, but are not as far along in holding positions of power in government as their educational attainment would suggest. Why is that so and what can be done about it? What can the United States learn from other countries?

- As organizations become more diverse and leaders arise from non-dominant groups, such as women, what will be the outcomes on mentoring relationships? What are the benefits to mentor, protégé, the organization?
- How can educational institutions such as school systems work to insure greater gender equality in the math and science performance of its students? How might more girls be encouraged to follow pursuits in science and technology?

What Makes the Present Different from the Past?

Looking back, we have seen from history that social change occurs slowly. If it has taken so long to arrive at the changes thus far, what does the future hold? Why should we believe that things will be different any time soon? Well, there are times when a society experiences an acceleration of the forces of change. We may be living in one of those times now. As discussed in Chapter 2, the period from the 1990s into the early twenty-first century has seen new inventions that have shrunk the world. Technology and globalization have altered the world of work. Generations X and Y have shown us just how adept we humans can be in communicating instantaneously with each other around the world. Women have more role models so they can visualize themselves being successful and say, "I can imagine myself being in that role." In a mere two-year timeframe we have witnessed a couple of "firsts" in political leadership: in 2007, the first woman became the Speaker of the House of Representatives; in 2008 the Democratic Party had a female candidate run in the presidential primary elections, and the Republican Party selected a woman candidate to run as Vice-President. When women have titles of CEO, President, Chief Financial Officer, Chief Information Officer, to name a few, there is a greater likelihood that the stereotypical perceptions that place limitations on men and women will erode over time.

Work–life issues are no longer considered just "women's issues." Men and women can partner together in achieving a new social contract. But inequalities in the workplace and in the home present different challenges for men and women. It is clear that gender and fairness issues must be addressed.

Hopefully, this book contributes to the ongoing dialogue that must occur as men and women in organizations work together to remove the barriers that women face in the labyrinth, to utilize their talents, and to solve work–life issues. Women and men are justified in asking the question, "What more can we do to ensure that organizations and society become more adaptive to our needs in the twenty-first century?"

Men and women will continue to seek ways to create meaningful lives for themselves, their families, and their communities. By applying our knowledge to that endeavor we can hope to flourish as individuals, and to create organizations and societies that engender in us a sense of purpose, satisfaction, and pride.

Notes

Preface

1 Valerio, 2006

Chapter 1

1 *Catalyst*, 2004

Chapter 2

1 Roth, 2006
2 Eagly & Carli, 2007
3 Morrison, White & Van Velsor, 1987
4 Valerio & Lee, 2005
5 Friedman, 2005
6 U.S. Bureau of Labor Statistics, 2006
7 Lewin, 2006
8 U.S. National Center for Education Statistics, 2006
9 Dreifus, 2008
10 Families and Work Institute, 2005
11 Families and Work Institute, 2005
12 Belkin, 2008
13 Hochschild, 1989
14 Belkin, 2008

Chapter 3

1 Frisch, 1998
2 Hyde, 2005

3 Schein, 2001
4 Heilman, Block, & Martell, 1995
5 Schmidt & Hunter, 2004
6 Eagly & Carli, 2007
7 John & Srivastava, 1999
8 Judge, Bono, Ilies, & Gerhardt, 2002
9 Costa, Terracciano, & McCrae, 2001
10 Eagly & Carli, 2007
11 Eagly & Carli, 2007
12 Spreier, Fontaine, & Malloy, 2006
13 Spreier, Fontaine, & Malloy, 2006
14 Eagly & Johnson, 1990
15 Burns, 1978
16 Eagly, Johannesen-Schmidt, & van Engen, 2003
17 Eagly & Carli, 2007
18 Ohlott, 2004
19 Van Velsor & Hughes-James, 1990
20 Lyness & Thompson, 2000
21 Corporate Leadership Council, 2001
22 Valerio & Lee, 2005
23 Kilburg, 2000
24 Kilburg, 2006
25 Valerio & Lee, 2005
26 Peterson, 2002
27 Ragins, 1999
28 Eby, Rhodes, & Allen, 2007
29 Ragins, 1999
30 Kram, 1996
31 Ragins, 1999
32 Eby, Rhodes, & Allen, 2007
33 Ragins, 2007
34 Bracken, Timmreck, & Church, 2001
35 Guthrie & King, 2004
36 Ruderman, 2004
37 Ohlott & Hughes-James, 1997

Chapter 4

1 Johnston & Packer, 1987
2 Ely & Foldy, 2003
3 *Catalyst*, 2004
4 Leonhardt, 2008

5 Reier, 2008

6 Kalev, Dobbin, & Kelly, 2006

7 Matza, 2008

8 Tarulli, 2008

9 Church, 2008

10 Church, Gallus, Desrosiers, & Waclawski, 2007

11 Corporate Leadership Council, 2005

12 Wellington, Kropf, & Gerkovich, 2003

13 Wellington, 2001

14 Lyness & Heilman, 2006

15 Kalev, Dobbin, & Kelly, 2006

16 Pedigo & Walsh, 2008

17 Tarulli, 2008

18 Roth, 2006

19 Cohen & D'Egidio, 2008

20 Deutsch, 2008

21 Valerio & Lee, 2005

22 Rosen, NY Times, 2006

23 Sutton & Noe, 2005

24 Benko & Weisberg, 2007

25 Benko & Weisberg, 2007

26 Adachi, 2008

27 Matza, 2008

28 Mass career customization is a U.S. patent pending process.

29 Adachi, 2008

Chapter 5

1 McCauley, 1986

2 Wood & Eagly, 2002

3 Valian, 1998

4 Ruderman & Ohlott, 2002

5 Eagly & Carli, 2007

6 Schein, 2001

7 Eagly & Carli, 2007

8 Eagly & Carli, 2007

9 Allen, 2006

10 *Catalyst*, 2007

11 Eagly & Carli, 2007

12 Eagly, Makhijani, & Klonsky, 1992

13 Eagly & Carli, 2007

14 Eagly & Carli, 2007

15 *Catalyst*, 2007
16 Rhode, 2003
17 Heilman, Block, & Martell, 1995
18 Lyness & Heilman, 2006
19 Lyness & Heilman, 2006
20 Morrison, White & Van Velsor, 1987
21 Eagly & Carli, 2007
22 Valerio & Lee, 2005
23 Wellington, Kropf, & Gerkovich, 2003
24 Lyness & Heilman, 2006
25 Ryan & Haslam, 2007
26 Carli, 2001
27 Albino, 2007

Chapter 6

1 Lee & King, 2001
2 Babcock & Laschever, 2003
3 Ragins, 1999
4 Ragins, 1999
5 Valerio & Lee, 2005

Chapter 8

1 Brizendine, 2006
2 Morrison, White, & Van Velsor, 1987
3 Eagly & Carli, 2007
4 Hewlett & Luce, 2005
5 Mainiero & Sullivan, 2006
6 Hewlett & Luce, 2005
7 Mainiero & Sullivan, 2006
8 Rhode & Kellerman, 2007
9 Thompson, Beauvais, & Allen, 2005

References and
Further Readings

Adachi, B. (2008, April 12). *Mass career customization: Retaining critical talent through creating options for everyone.* Paper presented at the 23rd Annual Conference of the Society for Industrial and Organizational Psychology, San Francisco.

Albino, J. E. (2007). Women as academic leaders: Living the experience from two perspectives. In J. L. Chin, B. Lott, J. K. Rice, & J. Sanchez-Hucles (Eds.), *Women and leadership: Transforming visions and diverse voices* (pp. 69–87). Malden, MA: Blackwell Publishing.

Allen, T. D. (2006). Rewarding good citizens: The relationship between citizenship behavior, gender, and organizational rewards. *Journal of Applied Social Psychology, 36*(1), 120–143.

Babcock, L., & Laschever, S. (2003). *Women don't ask: Negotiation and the gender divide.* Princeton, NJ: Princeton University Press.

Belkin, L. (2008, June 15). When mom and dad share it all. *The New York Times Magazine.* Retrieved June 16, 2008, from http://www.nytimes.com

Benko, C., & Weisberg, A. (2007). *Mass career customization: Aligning the workplace with today's nontraditional workforce.* Boston, MA: Harvard Business School Press.

Bracken, D. W., Timmreck, C. W., & Church, A. H. (Eds.). (2001). *The handbook of multi-source feedback.* San Francisco: Jossey-Bass.

Brizendine, L. (2006). *The female brain.* New York: Morgan Road Books.

Burns, J. M. (1978). *Leadership.* New York: Harper & Row.

Carli, L. L. (2001). Gender and social influence. *Journal of Social Issues, 57*(4), 725–741.

Catalyst. (2004). *The bottom line: Connecting corporate performance and gender diversity.* Retrieved January 3, 2008, from: http://catalyst.org/files/full/financialperformancereport.pdf

Catalyst. (2006). *2005 Catalyst census of women corporate officers and top earners of the Fortune 500*. Retrieved January 3, 2008, from: http://www.catalyst.org/files/full/2005%20COTE.pdf

Catalyst. (2007). *The double-bind dilemma for women in leadership: Damned if you do, doomed if you don't*. Retrieved April 24, 2008, from: http://www.catalystwomen.org/files/full/2007%20Double%20Bind.pdf

Church, A. H. Personal communication, May 28, 2008.

Church, A. H., Gallus, J. A., Desrosiers, E. I., & Waclawski, J. (2007). Speak-up all you whistle-blowers: An OD perspective on the impact of employee hotlines on organizational culture. *Organization Development Journal, 25*(4), 159–167.

Cohen, R., & D'Egidio, E. (2008, May 20). *Growing women leaders for the future*. Paper presented at the meeting of The Metropolitan Association of Applied Psychology, New York City.

Corporate Leadership Council. (2001). *Voice of the leader: A quantitative analysis of leadership bench strength and development strategies*. Washington, DC: Corporate Executive Board.

Corporate Leadership Council. (2005). *PepsiCo's dual performance rating practice: An overview of the practice and a conversation with Allan Church, Vice President of Organization and Management Development*. Washington, DC: Corporate Executive Board.

Costa, P. T. Jr., Terracciano, A., & McCrae, R. R. (2001). Gender differences in personality traits across cultures: Robust and surprising findings. *Journal of Personality and Social Psychology, 81*, 322–331.

Deutsch, C. H. (2008, March 26). Volunteering abroad to climb at IBM. *The New York Times*, C4. Retrieved March 27, 2008, from: http://www.nytimes.com

Dreifus, C. (2008, January 8). In professor's model, diversity=productivity. *The New York Times*, F2. Retrieved January 9, 2008, from: http://www.nytimes.com

Eagly, A. H., & Carli, L. L. (2007). *Through the labyrinth: The truth about how women become leaders*. Boston, MA: Harvard Business School Press.

Eagly, A. H., Johannesen-Schmidt, M. C, & van Engen, M. L. (2003). Transformational, transactional, and laissez-faire leadership styles: A meta-analysis comparing women and men. *Psychological Bulletin, 129*, 569–591.

Eagly, A. H. & Johnson, B. T. (1990). Gender and leadership style. *Psychological Bulletin, 108*, 233–256.

Eagly, A. H., Makhijani, M. G., & Klonsky, B. G. (1992). Gender and the evaluation of leaders: A meta-analysis. *Psychological Bulletin, 111*, 3–22.

Ely, R. J., & Foldy, E. G. (2003). Diversity: Overview. In R. J. Ely, E. G. Foldy, & M. A. Scully (Eds.), *Reader in gender, work and organization* (pp. 321–326). Malden, MA: Blackwell.

Eby, L. T., Rhodes, J. E., & Allen, T. D. (2007). Definition and evolution of mentoring. In T. D. Allen & L. T. Eby (Eds.), *The Blackwell handbook of mentoring: A multiple perspectives approach* (pp. 7–20). Malden, MA: Blackwell.

Families and Work Institute. (2005). *Generation and gender in the workplace.* Retrieved January 6, 2008, from http://familiesandwork.org/eproducts/genandgender.pdf

Fortune. (2007). *Fortune* 50 most powerful women in business. Retrieved November 15, 2007, from http://money.cnn.com/magazines/fortune/mostpowerfulwomen/2007/

Friedman, T. (2005). *The world is flat: A brief history of the 21st century.* New York: Farrar, Strauss, Giroux.

Frisch, M. H. (1998). Designing the individual assessment process. In R. Jeanneret & R. Silzer (Eds.), *Individual psychological assessment: Predicting behavior in organizational settings* (pp. 135–177). San Francisco: Jossey-Bass.

Guthrie, V. A., & King, S. N. (2004). Feedback-intensive programs. In C. D. McCauley & E. Van Velsor (Eds.), *The center for creative leadership handbook of leadership development* (pp. 25–57). San Francisco: Jossey-Bass.

Heilman, M. E., Block, C. J., & Martell, R. F. (1995). Sex stereotypes: Do they influence perceptions of managers? *Journal of Social Behavior and Personality, 10,* 237–252.

Hewlett, S. A., & Luce, C. B. (2005). Off-ramps and on-ramps: Keeping talented women on the road to success. *Harvard Business Review, 83*(3), 43–54.

Hochschild, A. R. (1989). *The Second Shift.* New York: Viking Penguin.

Hyde, J. S. (2005). The gender similarities hypothesis. *American Psychologist, 60*(6), 581–592.

John, O. P., & Srivastava, S. (1999). The big five trait taxonomy: History, measurement, and theoretical perspectives. In E. Pervin & O. John (Eds.), *Handbook of personality* (pp. 102–138). New York: Guilford Press.

Johnston, W. B., & Packer, A. E. (1987). *Workforce 2000: Work and workers for the twenty-first century.* Indianapolis, IN: Hudson Institute.

Judge, T. A., Bono, J. E., Ilies, R., & Gerhardt, M. W. (2002). Personality and leadership: A qualitative and quantitative review. *Journal of Applied Psychology, 87,* 765–780.

Kalev, A., Dobbin, F., & Kelly, E. (2006). Best practices or best guesses? Assessing the efficacy of corporate affirmative action and diversity policies. *American Sociological Review, 71,* 589–617.

Kilburg, R. R. (2000). *Executive coaching: Developing managerial wisdom in a world of chaos.* Washington, DC: American Psychological Association.

Kilburg, R. R. (2006). *Executive wisdom: Coaching and the emergence of virtual leaders.* Washington, DC: American Psychological Association.

Kram, K. (1996). A relational approach to career development. In D. T. Hall (Ed.), *The career is dead – long live the career: A relational approach to careers* (pp. 132–157). San Francisco: Jossey-Bass.

Lee, R. J., & King, S. N. (2001). *Discovering the leader in you: A guide to realizing your personal leadership potential.* San Francisco: Jossey-Bass.

Leonhardt, D. (2008, May 21). A diploma's worth? Ask her. *The New York Times.* Retrieved May 22, 2008, from: http://www.nytimes.com

Lewin, T. (2006, July 9). At colleges, women are leaving men in the dust. *The New York Times,* A1, A16, A17.

Lyness, K. S., & Heilman, M. E. (2006). When fit is fundamental: Performance evaluations and promotions of upper-level female and male managers. *Journal of Applied Psychology, 91*(4), 777–785.

Lyness, K. S., & Thompson, D. E. (2000). Climbing the corporate ladder: Do female and male executives follow the same route? *Journal of Applied Psychology, 85*(1), 86–101.

Mainiero, L. A., & Sullivan, S. E. (2006). *The opt-out revolt.* Mountain View, CA: Davies-Black Publishing.

Matza, R. (2008, May 20). *Deloitte women's initiative: Looking beyond the summit.* Paper presented at the meeting of The Metropolitan New York Association of Applied Psychology, New York City.

McCauley, C. D. (1986). *Developmental experiences in managerial work: A literature review.* [Technical Report 26]. Greensboro, NC: Center for Creative Leadership.

Morrison, A. M., White, R. P., & Van Velsor, E. (1987). *Breaking the glass ceiling.* Reading, MA: Addison-Wesley.

Ohlott, P. J. (2004). Job assignments. In C. D. McCauley & E. Van Velsor (Eds.), *The center for creative leadership handbook of leadership development* (pp. 151–182). San Francisco: Jossey-Bass.

Ohlott, P. J., & Hughes-James, M. W. (1997). Single-gender and single-race leadership development programs: Concerns and benefits. *Leadership in Action, 17*(4), 8–12.

Pedigo, P., & Walsh, S. (2008). *Using technology for global reach in developing women leaders: IBM's Super Women's Group.* Paper presented at the 23rd Annual Conference of The Society for Industrial and Organizational Psychology, San Francisco.

Peterson, D. B. (2002). Management development: Coaching and mentoring programs. In K. Kraiger (Ed.), *Creating, implementing and managing effective training and development* (pp. 160–191). San Francisco: Jossey-Bass.

Ragins, B. R. (1999). Gender and mentoring relationships: A review and research agenda for the next decade. In G. Powell (Ed.), *Handbook of gender and work* (pp. 347–370). Thousand Oaks, CA: Sage.

Ragins, B. R. (2007). Diversity and workplace mentoring relationships: A review and positive social capital approach. In T.D. Allen & L.T. Eby (Eds.), *The Blackwell handbook of mentoring: A multiple perspectives approach.* Malden, MA: Blackwell Publishing.

Reier, S. (2008, March 22). In Europe, women gain on boards. *The New York Times*, March 22, C4.

Rhode, D. L. (Ed.). (2003). *The difference difference makes: Women and leadership.* Stanford, CA: Stanford University Press.

Rhode, D. L., & Kellerman, B. (2007). Women and leadership: The state of play. In B. Kellerman & D. L. Rhode (Eds.), *Women and leadership: The state of play and strategies for change* (pp. 1–62). San Francisco: Jossey-Bass.

Rosen, E. (2006, May 26). Finding a way back to the law. *The New York Times.* Retrieved May 27, 2006 from: http://www.nytimes.com

Roth, L. M. (2006). *Selling women short: Gender inequality on Wall Street.* Princeton, NJ: Princeton University Press.

Ruderman, M. N. (2004). Leader development across gender. In C. D. McCauley & E. Van Velsor (Eds.), *The center for creative leadership handbook of leadership development* (pp. 271–303). San Francisco: Jossey-Bass.

Ruderman, M. N., & Ohlott, P. J. (2002). *Standing at the crossroads: Next steps for high-achieving women.* San Francisco: Jossey-Bass.

Ryan, M. K., & Haslam, S. A. (2007). The glass cliff: Exploring the dynamics surrounding the appointment of women to precarious leadership positions. *Academy of Management Review, 32*(2), 549–572.

Schein, V. (2001). A global look at psychological barriers to women's progress in management. *Journal of Social Issues, 57,* 675–688.

Schmidt, F. L., & Hunter, J. (2004). General mental ability in the world of work: Occupational attainment and job performance. *Journal of Personality and Social Psychology, 86,* 162–173.

Spreier, S. W., Fontaine, M. H., & Malloy, R. L. (2006, June). Leadership run amok: The destructive potential of overachievers. *Harvard Business Review, 84*(6), 72–82, 144.

Sutton, K. L., & Noe, R. A. (2005). Family-friendly programs and work–life integration: More myth than magic? In E. E. Kossek & S. J. Lambert (Eds.), *Work and life integration: Organizational, cultural, and individual perspectives* (pp. 151–169). Mahwah, NJ: Lawrence Erlbaum Associates.

Tarulli, B. (2008). *Engagement and retention of women at PepsiCo.* Paper presented at the 23rd Annual Conference of The Society for Industrial and Organizational Psychology, San Francisco.

Thompson, C. A., Beauvais, L. L., & Allen, T. A. (2005). Work–life balance: An industrial-organizational psychology perspective. In M. Pitt-Catsouphes, E. E., Kossek, & S. Sweet. (Eds.), *Work–family handbook*. Mahwah, NJ: Lawrence Erlbaum Associates.

U.S. Bureau of Labor Statistics. (2006). *Women in the labor force: A databook*. [Report 996]. Retrieved January 3, 2008, from: http://www.bls.gov/cps/wlf-databook2007.htm

U.S. National Center for Education Statistics. (2006). *Digest of education statistics*. Retrieved December 4, 2007, from: http://nces.ed.gov/programs/digest/d06/tables/dt06_251.asp?referrer=list

Valerio, A. M. (2006) An action plan for developing women leaders. *Leadership in Action, 26*(5), 16–19. San Francisco: Center for Creative Leadership & Wiley & Sons.

Valerio, A. M., & Lee, R. J. (2005) *Executive coaching: A guide for the HR professional*. San Francisco: John Wiley & Sons.

Valian, V. (1998). *Why so slow? The advancement of women*. Cambridge, MA: MIT Press.

Van Velsor, E., & Hughes-James, M. W. (1990). *Gender differences in the development of managers: How women managers learn from experience*. Greensboro, NC: Center for Creative Leadership.

Wellington, S. (2001). *Be your own mentor: Strategies from top women on the secrets of success*. New York: Random House.

Wellington, W., Kropf, M. B., & Gerkovich, P. R. (2003). What's holding women back? *Harvard Business Review, 81*(6), 18–19.

Wood, W., & Eagly, A. H. (2002). A cross-cultural analysis of the behavior of women and men: Implications for the origins of sex differences. *Psychological Bulletin, 128*(5), 699–727.

Name Index

Subject Index